THE
WINNER'S
MIND

A Competitor's Guide To
Sports and Business Success

By Allen Fox, Ph.D.

Racquet Tech Publishing
An Imprint of the USRSA
Vista, California, USA

USRSA
330 Main St.
Vista, California 92084
www.racquettech.com

Library of Congress Control Number: 2004097928

Printed in the United States of America

ISBN 0-9722759-2-4

To Nancy, my incredible wife, and to Evan and Charlie, my beautiful sons.

Thanks to my loving family, my home is, to me, the happiest place on earth. Without emotional turmoil, concentrating on writing the book was easy. Nancy is the most gentle, thoughtful, giving person I have ever met, so she forms the basis for my happy existence. Everywhere she is becomes a pleasant refuge from the stress and competitiveness of the outside world. And her happy genetics and daily influence have produced two bright, well-balanced, and nice kids. What more could I ask for?

TABLE
OF
CONTENTS

PART ONE
THE COMPULSION TO COMPETE AND ACHIEVE

CHAPTER ONE
THE MIND OF THE HABITUAL WINNER   3

Successful people in any area have certain common mental characteristics. This chapter analyzes the personality types of the great competitors and habitual winners, as well as the genetic and environmental factors that produce them. These individuals make up only a small percentage of the population, yet they are successful at whatever they undertake, whether it is sports, business, the professions, or academics.

CHAPTER TWO
WHY DO WE HUNGER TO WIN?   15

The drive to win—to achieve and be successful—is, to an important degree, determined genetically. We focus on the work of Konrad Lorenz, whose studies suggest that, like other species, our drives for territory, sex, and position on the social hierarchy are the most powerful innate underpinnings of our drive to win.

CHAPTER THREE
HOW SOCIETY PRESSURES US TO WIN   35

This chapter explores the environmental factors such as societal and parental influences that cause us to want to win. It becomes clear, after the first three chapters, that our desires to win and become successful are powerful, universal, and determined by both heredity and environment.

CHAPTER FOUR
THE INSIDIOUS AND PERVASIVE FEAR OF FAILURE   45

Now the dark side of the achievement equation appears. All competition and drives for achievement are accompanied by the fear of failure. Though often unconscious, this fear is powerful and pervasive and is always a factor in competition. Although it can, at times, be motivational and even positive, it more often hinders one's ability to achieve. In order to reach one's full achievement potential, fear of failure must be faced and overcome.

CHAPTER FIVE
THE UNCONSCIOUS STRUGGLE
BETWEEN AMBITION AND FEAR   57

Fear of failure is usually unconscious and interferes directly with the drive for achievement, causing most people to become inefficient competitors. Fear nullifies much of the competitor's will to win and distorts the competitor's perceptions. Its destructive effects cause people to refuse to compete, lie to themselves, make excuses, blame others for their failures, repudiate and replace their real goals with goals easier to achieve, fail to finish tasks, procrastinate difficult tasks, and panic on the verge of victory.

PART TWO
HOW THE CHAMPIONS DO IT

INTRODUCTION TO PART TWO   69

CHAPTER SIX
GOAL ORIENTATION   71

This chapter is about goal setting. The successful identify clear long-term goals and develop game plans for reaching them. This leads to a succession of short-term goals upon which the successful focus their energies. Without such plans, important tasks become frightening and confusing. This chapter discusses short- and long-term goals, game plans, and how to focus one's energies more productively.

CHAPTER SEVEN
KEEPING GOALS IN MIND   87

High achievers never forget to keep their eyes on the ball. Any actions they take are calculated to lead them toward (and never away from) their goals. They only do things that help them win. The losers, by contrast, often act contrary to their own interests. Examples of this are when they argue with customers in a retail situation, fail to complete tasks in the workplace, or become angry or discouraged in athletic contests.

CHAPTER EIGHT
THE FEELING OF CONTROL 97

The winners subconsciously feel as if they can control the outcome of events themselves. This makes them take responsibility for success or failure. It makes them work harder and more persistently to win. The losers think that success or failure is determined by factors outside of their control, and they are, therefore, susceptible to excuses, passivity, and weakness.

CHAPTER NINE
A SOLUTION TO ANY PROBLEM 105

The winners subconsciously believe that all problems can be solved. This assumption inspires them to overcome difficulties. A roadblock simply causes them to search through multiple alternative solutions until they find one that works.

CHAPTER TEN
SENSITIVITY TO SUCCESS 115

The winners have a sharp eye for what is working and what is not. They learn quickly from success and failure. Like sharks to blood, they are immediately attracted to approaches that are successful and just as quickly repelled by approaches that are not. The losers, on the other hand, appear almost oblivious to the effectiveness or lack thereof of their achievement strategies.

CHAPTER ELEVEN
REACTION TO FAILURE 125

Losses simply make the champions more determined to win. Undaunted, they increase their preparations and efforts so that on subsequent attempts they can improve their odds of success. By contrast, failure discourages those with the loser's mentality. Disheartened, they reduce their efforts and become increasingly likely to lose and, ultimately, quit.

CHAPTER TWELVE
CAPACITY FOR WORK 135

The ability to work harder and longer than other people is, in itself, a talent. It can often outweigh intelligence, formal education, and a host of other mental and physical talents in the quest for success.

CHAPTER THIRTEEN
Work Without Immediate Reward 143

Most people can work hard for short periods of time if they are rewarded quickly and handsomely. Otherwise, they are likely to lose heart and give up. By contrast, the champions are tough and have the long view. They can see past the valley to the hill beyond and can work without reward as long as necessary to reach their goals.

CHAPTER FOURTEEN
Intellect Over Emotion 151

Man is seldom the rational being in practice that he is in theory. In fact, most people use their logic systems to back up their emotions rather than the other way around. The winners do not fall into this trap. With them practicality and goal orientation take precedence over counterproductive emotions.

CHAPTER FIFTEEN
Energy 161

The winners have extraordinary physical and mental energy. They are up early and in motion. They are relentless and determined to reach their goals. They are willing to delegate tasks to others, but only reluctantly. They would do everything themselves if they could, but realize that they can't, so they delegate. By contrast, the less successful lack force and energy. They are slow and reluctant to move and happily hand off tasks to others because they don't want to do them themselves.

CHAPTER SIXTEEN
What Does It All Mean? 175

Of course winning is far better than losing, but at the same time our drives to win and achieve are only parts of our psychological makeup. We need, above all, intelligent balance in our lives. Although it is difficult to be happy without at least some measure of achievement and competitive success, it is equally or more difficult without friends and a congenial family life.

APPENDIX 179

ABOUT THE AUTHOR 189

Acknowledgments

I am greatly in debt to a number of people who were instrumental in helping me shape the book into its final form. Mark Winters and Joel Drucker, great writers in their own right, took their valuable time to read and offer insightful criticism. My brilliant brother, Michael Fox, pointed out weaknesses that have since been corrected as per his detailed instructions. Leslie Epstein, a genius who teaches creative writing at Boston College and has written a dozen highly acclaimed books, gave me heartwarming encouragement. My closest friends, Richard Mosk, George Zwerdling, Herb FitzGibbon, and Larry Nagler didn't do a darn thing for the book, but since I like them so much, I felt obliged to mention them. And last, but hardly least, is Crawford Lindsey, my clever Ivy League publisher and editor. If he had not had confidence in me, I would have had to e-mail each of you a copy of this book.

PART ONE

THE COMPULSION
TO COMPETE
AND ACHIEVE

This book is about competition and its first cousin, achievement. It will explain what drives us to compete and achieve, what the difficulties are, and how anyone can become more successful at it.

WHAT IS INCLUDED IN PART ONE?

The first five chapters comprise Part One and are intended to give the reader a deeper understanding of why we are driven to compete and achieve. They explore what we are really up to when we try to win athletic contests, live in nicer houses, wear Rolex watches, write books, give our words extra weight in social situations, do scientific research, and the myriad of other occupations and pastimes that make up the complex game of life. Of course, desiring success in these areas is only part of the equation. Everyone wants to be successful. Only a few are consistently successful. So these chapters also lay bare the emotional roadblocks that hinder so many people in their quest for success and help us to correct our own counterproductive behaviors that lead to failure.

THE PURPOSE OF USING EXAMPLES FROM SPORTS

Why, when I am really interested in generalized competition, do I use so many examples from sports? Because the elements that lead to success or failure in sport are the same as those that lead to success or failure in any other area of endeavor. In sports these elements are easy to see and understand because they take place in a short time and in a confined area. Business is different. The same mechanisms operate, but their results may not surface for years and their outcomes are not so clear. In sports, you simply, in a matter of minutes, or at most a few hours, win or lose. There is nowhere to hide, and responsibility for success or failure is clear.

WHY ARE EXAMPLES FROM TENNIS PARTICULARLY USEFUL?

I tend to use examples from tennis more often than examples from other sports, and I do so for a number of reasons. First, tennis is an individual sport, so there is no shared responsibility. Winning or losing rests primarily with the players themselves, and a look into their minds will tell us very simply what helps or hurts performance. Second, the players are on the court all by themselves and for a relatively long time. This allows us to watch the competitive process evolve and the stresses build as the players struggle with a myriad of physical, mental, and emotional obstacles. The players' responses and actions are more clearly on display here than in the melee of a football or basketball game. Third, the personality characteristics necessary to become a successful tennis player are the same as those leading to success in any area.

Tennis is the sport I know the most about. I played tournaments my whole young life, and, with mediocre physical talent but exceptional competitive skills, I ultimately became one of the best players in the world, reaching the quarterfinals at Wimbledon and playing Davis Cup for the United States.

WHERE DID I LEARN ABOUT SUCCESS STRATEGIES?

I earned my Ph.D. in psychology from UCLA while playing tournament tennis at a world-class level. When my tennis career was over, I went into the investment business, ultimately running my own investment company. This and the several successful small businesses that I owned and ran afterward gave me first-hand knowledge of the factors leading to success and failure in business. All this, including my years of experience as a college tennis coach, has given me a deep, gut-level understanding of the competitive process. I do not speak simply as a psychologist when I suggest solutions to particular competitive problems, but from personal knowledge as well. These ideas worked for me, and they can also work for you. Equally important, I know what approaches don't work, having tried them myself and experienced, unfortunately, my share of losses.

THE MIND
OF THE
HABITUAL WINNER

Successful people have certain common
mental characteristics that help them to be
successful in any area of endeavor.

Searing heat saps the strength from the combatants on the center court of the Foro Italico Stadium in Rome. It is 1961 and the opening match is underway in the Davis Cup between Italy and the United States. Young Jon Douglas of Santa Monica, California, trails famed Italian star Fausto Gardini two sets to none. Fausto has been a fearsome force on the slow Europeon clay courts for the past 10 years, particularly in Italy where he is a maestro at whipping partisan crowds into an emotional frenzy. They are screaming today as Fausto gives Douglas a tennis lesson. Pounding his big forehand to the corners and teasing Douglas with skidding slices and deft dropshots off the backhand, Fausto has been toying with the Californian for hours. Douglas had learned his tennis on the fast concrete courts of Los Angeles and is obviously below par and uncomfortable on Rome's slippery red dirt.

But Douglas lowers his head and doggedly continues to run and fight. He understands that he cannot master the intricacies of this alien surface in the next hours. The race does not always go to the swiftest. Youthful and tough, Douglas realizes his only chance is to scramble for every ball and try to keep the older Gardini on the hot court until he tires. Douglas is prepared to run two miles just to make Fausto run one.

The third set goes to the American 7–5, and the fourth turns into a marathon. With the score standing at 8–all (there were no tie-breakers in those days) and after almost four hours on court, Fausto begins to wilt. A little weariness of leg is all Douglas needs to close out the set 10–8. Now they are even and Fausto knows he is finished. Indicating to the now silent and sullen crowd that he is starting to get cramps, Fausto puts up only token resistance in the deciding set, which Douglas wins without the loss of a game. It is a fitting end to a match that is a high point in Jon Douglas' tennis career and exemplifies his approach to tennis, other sports, and life in general. Quite simply, Jon Douglas knows how to win.

THE DOUGLAS STORY

Jon Douglas is a good example of a competitive genius. He was ranked as high as number four in tennis in the United States and was a valued member of the U.S. Davis Cup team in the early 1960s. He graduated from Stanford University and, while he was at it, played first-string quarterback on their football team. Not content with mediocrity in any sport, Douglas was one of the best quarterbacks in the league—so good that in post-season play he was named quarterback for the West team in the annual East-West game and almost won the game single-handedly by passing for one touchdown and running for two others. And that was not the end of his accomplishments. While playing football and tennis at Santa Monica High School and accumulating close to an A average academically, he found the time to play first-string basketball, and earn All-Bay League honors!

Douglas was the top junior tennis player in Southern California and one of the best in the nation when I moved to California as a 16-year old. It was not long before I began to hear the stories about him. Because he was so successful at so many sports, his achievements were the stuff of legend. Never having met Douglas, I naturally pictured him to be a powerful, bionic athlete, with eagle eyes and superhuman coordination.

DOUGLAS DIDN'T DO IT WITH ATHLETIC ABILITY

What a surprise when I finally saw him. I felt like Dorothy meeting the Wizard of Oz. Douglas was singularly unimpressive as a physical specimen. At five feet nine inches and 155 pounds, he was terribly disadvantaged in both football and basketball. More surprising still was the fact that he was not a particularly gifted physical athlete in any other measurable characteristic either. His hand-eye coordination was only average, and though tough, he was not terribly strong. Possessed of excellent quickness and balance, he was a good but certainly not great athlete.

As a basketball player, he was an excellent ball handler, but only a fair shot. He had no fancy moves but he was quick, strong on defense, a clever passer, and always in the right place. He was valuable to his team because he seldom made mistakes and had a knack for causing his opponents difficulty. He was constantly alert to break up their plays and steal balls while maneuvering his teammates into the open for easy shots.

In football he was similarly efficient but unspectacular. Douglas did not have a strong passing arm but was quite accurate at short range. He was a wonderful field general and excellent at option plays and scrambling. He passed at the right times, found the holes in the defense, and had the foresight to stay out of trouble. But he was incapable of heaving the ball significant distances effectively or wiggling free of multiple tacklers to gain yardage. So he simply didn't try to do these things.

The format in tennis was much the same. Douglas was not at all gifted with the racquet, but he was an excellent mechanic. Although his strokes looked a little stiff, they were well practiced and reliable. He employed his fine backhand, consistent baseline game, and superior conditioning to wear opponents down. His serve was mediocre and his volley, an afterthought. What didn't show was his incredible intellect and competitive heart.

Douglas was not a good enough physical athlete to become great in any of his sports. But he was truly exceptional in having the instinct for using his strengths to maximum advantage, hiding his weaknesses, and competing with ferocious intensity. Without doubt he could have achieved national prominence in baseball, hockey, soccer, water polo, or tiddlywinks if he had set his mind to it.

DOUGLAS TURNS TO BUSINESS

After finishing his athletic career, Douglas turned his considerable energies toward making money. He entered the real estate business as a broker, nothing fancy, just selling real estate like hordes of other brokers. But before long he was selling a lot more real estate than they were. Over the years, he built a solid base of knowledge and contacts. Eventually he began to syndicate partnerships to purchase or develop income property. Douglas knew what he was talking about, and people listened to him. Before long he opened his own real estate brokerage firm, the Jon Douglas Company, which, in time, developed into a behemoth. It became the largest and most respected brokerage firm in Southern California before he sold it in 1997 to the national public brokerage firm of Coldwell-Banker. Now, Douglas is an incredibly wealthy man, with mountains of cash and extensive holdings of valuable Southern California real estate. Clearly, whatever mental qualities are entailed in the art of successful competition, Douglas has them.

WINNING MENTALITIES WORK IN ALL ARENAS

As Douglas' career suggests, the mental traits involved in achievement and success appear transferable from one sport to another and to business as well. They are generalized attitudes and mental approaches to problem solving that certain individuals employ in whatever realm they wish to become successful. These individuals are rare. Relatively few people are innately excellent competitors. Fortunately, the rest of us can learn how to do it by observing, analyzing, and emulating the tricks used by those that are naturally good at it.

ONLY A FEW ARE NATURALS

A study on fighter pilots in World War II showed that approximately five percent of the pilots accounted for virtually all the enemy planes that were shot down. And what was the other 95 percent doing meanwhile? They were getting shot down by the 5 percent of the enemy pilots that were accounting for all of our losses. Now there is a sport where it pays to be good. Lose and you get killed.

The interesting thing is how so few of the pilots were doing all of the damage. These 5 percent were the great competitors. They had, somehow, figured out how to become excellent in this particular little realm, and they far surpassed the great majority of other pilots. Most of them would have done a disproportionate amount of winning if the competitive arena had been tennis, golf, football, business, or even monopoly.

On the other hand, most people do not naturally compete well and manage to get beaten by the great competitors, whenever or wherever they encounter them. This book's objective is to help the average reader identify his or her own competitive weaknesses and fix them. To do this, the reader will need to gain a deeper understanding of the underlying elements that drive and inhibit one's ability to compete—a necessary first step because so many of the roadblocks to success are unconscious. Like many psychological difficulties, bringing them into the open helps us to conquer them. Afterward, we will hone in on the specific techniques that champions use to achieve their ends, so we can proceed to use them ourselves.

THE WINNER'S SKILLS WORK ANYWHERE

Douglas is not unusual in his ability to transfer his competitive skills from one sport to another or from athletics to business. For example, most of the higher ranked American tennis players of my day eventually left sports and made their marks in business or the professions. This was because, in the 1960s, there was little money to be made in tennis. Although we played all the major tournaments such as Wimbledon and the US, French, and Australian Championships, the amateur officials controlled the game and there was no prize money. We were paid "expense" money, which was a code word for all the under-the-table cash you were able to negotiate out of thrifty tournament directors. We all loved the excitement of competition and travel but realized that we would have to make our livings elsewhere.

The highly ranked players who went into business, almost without exception, made large amounts of money. And by "large amounts," I mean annual incomes of between hundreds of thousands of dollars and over a million. Several, like Dick Savitt (Wimbledon champion), Mike Franks (US Davis Cup player), Hamilton Richardson (ranked #1 in the US), and Herb FitzGibbon (reached the final 16 at both Wimbledon and the French Championships) made hefty fortunes in the investment business. Clark Graebner (finalist at the US Open) became extremely prosperous in the financial printing business. Jan Leshley (semi-finalist in the US Championship) became President of Squibb-Beech Corp. Larry Nagler, my old doubles partner at UCLA, has his own law firm and lives in a big house with a tennis court in Beverly Hills.

This relatively small group of top-ranked players, almost to the man, became conspicuously successful outside of tennis. The probability of this happening on strictly a chance basis is astronomically small. Clearly some factors relating to their success on the tennis courts was active. And it was not fame or personal contacts. In those days, tennis was a small game, and the players were not celebrities. They certainly knew wealthy people and could get a foot in the door on a personal basis, but that did not carry them far. It was what they did once they got in the door that distinguished them. Plenty of other people, by one means or another, get a foot in the door. But they don't succeed with this regularity.

THE MIND OF THE WINNER

Assuming there are some mental traits that allow some few people to surpass the ordinary herd in achievement, one may then question whether these people think alike in some manner? If so, are the mentalities of successful business people similar to those of successful athletes? In setting out to answer these questions, I administered personality tests to 26 highly ranked tennis professionals and compared the results to known personality profiles of successful business people.

Since one's personality is largely determined by genetics and early upbringing, I recognize that the reader will not be able to change his or her personality to fit the group norms of the champions. Nonetheless, this information is interesting because it shows that there is more than a chance correspondence between the personality characteristics of successful people in both business and sports. And this need not be discouraging to those readers who have different personality profiles. Part Two is designed to teach anyone to use the winning techniques that the champions seem to employ so naturally.

The test I administered was called the Cattell 16 PF test and, with 180 questions, measures certain "personality factors." Each factor is measured along a continuum such as suspicious-trusting, dominant-submissive, anxious-calm. They were by no means all the same mentally, but there were several characteristics in which, as a group, they showed statistically significant differences from the average.

As a group they tended to be, significantly more than the average person, suspicious, antagonistic, intelligent, dominant, and anxious. Although I did not test John McEnroe, Lleyton Hewitt, Jimmy Connors, or Jon Douglas, I know most of them well enough personally or have observed them closely enough to feel that they also fit this profile nicely. All four are bright, aggressive and quick to become antagonistic. Douglas, the most controlled and socially adept of the three, does not appear as anxious or aggressive as the others, but that is only because he has honed his interpersonal skills during his many years of experience as a businessman.

Of course this does not mean that all the players tested were suspicious or anxious or intelligent or dominant. Many were trusting or relaxed or less intelligent or submissive, yet they became great players too. So it is obviously possible for people with various personality profiles to become great players and champions. My statements only refer to group averages compared to the norms. Andre Agassi, for example, does not have the aggressive, antagonistic personality referred to above, yet he became a champion anyway. A great physical talent but a gentle soul—not naturally a great competitor—Agassi struggled early in his career to maintain drive and discipline. Weak competitive instincts led him to throw away a multitude of important matches that he could have won. Later he simply learned from his mistakes, changed his behavior, and became a fine competitor and consistent winner.

Why might characteristics like anxiety, antagonism, and suspicion be useful to a tournament tennis player? Anxiety, for example, would cause small issues to jangle their nervous systems and set off alarm bells to stimulate action. These people are not placid and sedentary. Anxiety would simply increase their motivation and, combined with their other personality traits, incite them to practice and work toward improvement.

Suspicion can also be useful in competitive tennis. Suspicious (paranoid would be the extreme case) people think that others are out to get the best of them or do them wrong. In an ambiguous situation, they immediately suspect the other person of evil intentions. They look at others as antagonists rather than allies, and they are quick to take steps to protect themselves. They are happy to get even with people they feel have wronged them. It is useful on the tennis court because these types of people aren't going to give their opponents the satisfaction of winning. After two or three hours grinding under a hot sun, normal people may question whether winning the match is all that necessary and, in fact, really worth the cost. People viewing their opponents as enemies have extra drive and cannot abide seeing them win. This drives them to do whatever it takes to win themselves. And if they lose, they plot revenge. They are motivated to practice extra hours and strive with renewed vigor to get better so this does not happen again. Losing to one's enemies is too painful to bear gracefully.

In less personally antagonistic sports, a modicum of paranoia can also be motivating. Ice skating champion Michelle Kwan was once quoted as saying, "It's good to have a rival, to have someone pushing you, helping keep you in line. [There are] those days you skate badly or you're too tired and you just want to climb in bed. But you think, 'I know she's out there working hard right now. I'd better get back to it.'"

THE PERSONALITY PROFILE IN ACTION

I have seen these traits in action at close range since I have them myself. For instance, one evening many years ago my close friend and ex-doubles partner, Larry Nagler, invited me to his home for dinner. He had a pool table, and after dinner, he induced me into a game. Larry had played a lot of pool, so he was pretty good at the game. I had never played, so I, of course, was terrible. Pool is a tricky game. Unless you hit the ball perfectly, it is very hard to control. Long shots are nearly impossible for novices, and the only balls you can make at this stage are balls right next to the hole. Being as competitive as he is, Larry was having a wonderful time toying with me. We played straight pool, and Larry spotted me 20 balls out of 25 and still beat me. All the while he laughed and chided me. By the end, my stomach was in knots, and I silently vowed revenge.

It so happened that at the end of the street where I lived, there was a pool hall. Every day after work I stopped there and spent two hours clandestinely practicing pool. I bought a book by Willie Mosconi, a legendary pool champion, and learned about proper technique. I was focused and diligent. After three months I had gotten pretty good. I could consistently run four or five balls at a stretch and make almost any shot of medium difficulty. Although Larry was still better than me, I now felt ready for a rematch.

Another dinner was scheduled at Larry's, and, afterward, I suggested a little pool. To make it interesting, I proposed that he again spot me 20 balls but that we place a few dollars wager on the outcome. Larry agreed with a chuckle and a superior look. He was not chuckling quite so much when I won that game with my new controlled and deliberate style. The next game he spotted me fifteen balls, and I won again. Now I was smiling, and Larry was getting a little hot. (Larry is almost as competitive as I am and not a happy loser.) He gave me a ten ball spot in the third game, and I won it with a smirk on my face deliberately designed to rub in my victory. By this time Larry was frustrated beyond endurance. I quit (because he was still better than me, and with any less than a 10 ball spot, I would have lost) and demanded immediate payment. With shirt buttons straining to hold his bulging neck, he said he would be happy to pay, but first I would have to fight him for the money. (What a sore loser!) Of course this type of drive, when channeled properly, provides a tremendous competitive advantage.

Is it necessary to have this personality profile in order to be successful, and are those people who differ doomed to be at a competitive disadvantage? Of course not. It is just that this particular personality profile often leads its possessors to naturally employ behavior patterns that help them win. Many people with other personality profiles also use the same behavior patterns, so they are successful competitors too. The difference between the groups is that a higher percentage of the first group behaves this way innately as compared to the other groups. Moreover, if it is not part of your genetic makeup to automatically employ successful behavior strategies, you can, as many people eventually do, simply learn how to do it and then employ these strategies by conscious effort of will.

THE "TYPE A" PERSONALITY

This same personality profile has been found in other groups of people. Drs. Rosenman and Friedman, in their groundbreaking work on the relationship between temperament and heart disease, described the famous "Type A" personality, which was virtually identical to the personality profile I found in championship tennis players. Type A individuals are aggressive, anxious, goal and achievement oriented, have difficulty relaxing, and have a layer of antagonism and aggressiveness towards other people smoldering just below the surface. (Sounds a lot like John McEnroe.) Significantly, they noted a strikingly large number of successful business executives among the Type A individuals that they interviewed, lending weight to the thesis that similar types of people tend to be successful in both business and sport.

Along these lines, I was talking with Richard Riordan (before he became the mayor of Los Angeles and an unsuccessful candidate for governor of California), who is an attorney, a successful businessman, and an extremely clever investor in emerging companies. I asked him if he could identify any particular trait or traits that were common to the leading business executives that he knew. Almost without a pause, he replied, "Paranoia." He said this keeps them driven, alert, and one jump ahead of the competition. And Andrew Grove, legendary former CEO of Intel, agrees with Riordan. His stated business mantra was, "Only the paranoid survive."

MESOMORPHS ALSO FIT THE PROFILE

In the early part of this century psychologist W. Sheldon described this personality type in yet another context. He was interested in a correspondence between body type and personality. His contention was that people with particular physical characteristics also tended to demonstrate distinctive mental characteristics or temperaments. When I read about this many years ago, I thought it had a hokey and unscientific ring. Why, I wondered, should a person's physical makeup have any relationship to his personality type? Since Sheldon's assertions were unproven and merely the result of his personal observations, my bent toward scientific rigor gave me qualms about accepting them. Now I am not so sure about such qualms. You, as the reader, can be the judge.

Sheldon divided people into three basic groups: mesomorphs, endomorphs, and ectomorphs. He described each group both physically and temperamentally, recognizing as he did so that many people fell between groups and that the dividing line between groups was inexact. Nonetheless, Sheldon insisted that these basic groups were distinct and identifiable.

Sheldon depicted mesomorphs as strong and muscular, contrasting with ectomorphs, who were slender and artistic, and endomorphs, who were soft, corpulent, rounded, and savored bodily pleasures. His temperamental profile of the mesomorph was almost identical to the Type A personality and the championship level tennis player. They were characterized as aggressive, dominant, competitive, and pugnacious. His descriptions were very detailed and even portrayed how they ate, which was "quickly and in a wolf-like manner." This contrasted with endomorphs, who savored their food and ectomorphs who were not overly interested in food.

As a competitive tennis player myself, the mesomorph description fit me with uncanny accuracy, both physically and mentally, even down to my manner of eating. Now, with the results of my personality tests on tennis champions in hand, along with the Type A personality information, I am inclined to take Sheldon more seriously.

It seems that there is, among us, an identifiable group of people that can be described as muscular, aggressive, anxious, pugnacious, and suspicious of others—traits that are likely genetic in origin (see Appendix 1). Moreover, this group is unusually successful in both sports and business. This is interesting because it provides some small measure of hard evidence that people with one particular set of mental characteristics are particularly effective competitors in two totally different realms. It suggests that the mental techniques that they use with such effectiveness in sport and business might also be effective in other areas of competition and achievement as well.

Assuming that there are some people that are particularly adept at competing in any area, that they may have certain similarities of personality, and even that they use similar techniques to achieve their ends, how will this help the rest of us to compete and achieve more successfully?

First, we will, in the next four chapters, explore the forces that drive us to compete, as well as the fears that hinder our effectiveness. Understanding these will allow us to make sense of our own effective and ineffective approaches to competition, a first step in virtually any psychological betterment processes. Once alerted to this information, we can consciously choose to make needed changes. And the ten chapters that come after that will provide specific tools for improving one's effectiveness as a competitor and achiever by identifying the ten most important techniques used by champions in sport, business, and elsewhere.

WHY DO WE HUNGER TO WIN?

Genetically determined drives for territory, sex, and position in the social hierarchy are the most powerful innate underpinnings of the drive to win.

Sports competition is a microcosm of competition in life. People have often questioned whether winning really matters. After all, sports are only games, and we generally distinguish games and play from activities that obviously matter, like jobs. People think games are pastimes and we engage in them only for fun, while jobs are real because they put bread on the table, clothes on our backs, and provide shelter for our families. That appears to be a valid distinction, but deeper analysis shows that the two are much the same. Donald Trump illustrated this when he said, "Money was never a big motivation for me, except as a way to keep score. The real excitement is playing the game." Jobs are mostly about competing and winning, just like sports.

WHAT ABOUT FEEDING OUR FAMILIES?

Jobs are more concerned with status than they are about putting bread on the table. In the United States, subsistence is not an issue. We are not going to starve to death if we lose our present job and have to settle for one with lower pay and less prestige. We might be embarrassed or feel disgraced, but we would still eat and have a roof over our heads. Most of the items we buy have little to do with subsistence or need and a great deal to do with status and the immediate pleasure we get from buying and accumulating things. We covet fancier cars and homes, more fashionable clothes, the most up-to-date computer, and knick-knacks of all kinds. The average home literally bulges with items that we want but do not need. Having them just makes us feel good. And we work our lives away to pay for them.

I once spent a month on the Gold Coast in Australia with my wife and young son. We rented a one-bedroom condominium near the beach and had a marvelous time sightseeing, swimming, playing tennis, and just living. Back in the United States, we had left a home full of possessions. Our closets were full of clothes, our cupboards and kitchen cabinets were packed with utensils, dishes, fine china, and crystal. Our drawers and shelves were filled with papers, mementos, and gadgets of all kinds—the accumulation of years of gifts and purchases. In fact, the house was literally overflowing with THINGS. We hardly had enough room left over for ourselves, yet there seemed to be nothing there that we could bear to get rid of. But in Australia, we were living quite happily in the little condominium with only one suitcase each. We could have lived there indefinitely without ever missing the contents of our closets, drawers, shelves, and cupboards back home. It is enough to make us question more deeply what our jobs are really meant to accomplish. (Could they be simply to satisfy our inner packrat?)

Another example came to mind some years ago during a visit to a factory where they made spray hoses for kitchen sinks. These are the little pull-out hoses that divert faucet water to clean off the sides of the sink. They look simple but in actuality are terribly complex. They contain a multitude of beautifully engineered little parts that had to be manufactured to minute tolerances. This required sophisticated machinery to bend and cut metal and mold plastics. Hundreds of workers were putting pieces together in an assembly line to form the end product. Everything was running like clockwork. Production standards and schedules were set and met. Graphs were on the walls, production meetings were held, plans were made, and the organization was superb.

This little factory, with its machinery, intelligence, efficiency, and 300 workers, was able to turn out several million of these devices per year and supply the needs of virtually the entire country. By comparison, if a device of this complexity had to be made in earlier times by one man alone in a workshop without the benefit of all this machinery and technology, it would have taken him a month to fashion just one of them. Our ability to produce tremendous quantities of things has expanded to undreamed of heights in the last fifty years. I pondered this as I watched the workers bustle about their jobs with relentless energy for days on end. Even with this great improvement in productive capacity, the workers were still working as hard as they could all day long. They had no more leisure time than they ever had. What, I asked myself, was the purpose of all this striving?

To answer this question, I imagined the factory down the street where another 300 workers were grinding away making ashtrays, fancy door handles, corkscrews, place mats, candlestick holders, or any of the million other gadgets and items that fill our closets, drawers, and shelves. These are all things that people want but don't need. In fact, no one really needs kitchen spray hoses either. But 300 people slave away all day making these spray hoses that no one needs to earn enough money to buy ashtrays, place mats, candlestick holders, and other gadgets that they don't need. Meeting our real needs for food, clothing, and shelter requires only a small part of the nation's greatly expanded productive output. The rest goes to meet the requirements of the other games that we are playing.

So why then are we really working at our jobs or competing in sports? We do so because we are genetically programmed to compete, achieve, and acquire. In addition, we are taught to do so by our parents and society. Whether we like it or not, we all want to win. We want to prevail in all aspects of achievement and two of these happen to be jobs and sports. Possessions and money are just ways of keeping score. We try to win in sports and be successful in business because winning and success, due to both our genetics and environment, make us feel good.

CAN'T WE JUST STOP TRYING SO HARD?

Some years ago, Tim Gallwey wrote a book about the mental side of tennis called *The Inner Game of Tennis,* which became the best selling book ever written on tennis. He postulated that winning was not the proper object of competition and that sportsmen would be better off enjoying the process of playing (such as the feel of hitting the ball) rather than focusing on techniques, goals, and winning. It was an anticompetitive book and its message was that winning didn't matter. This was well received in the 1970s when antiestablishment thinking was the rage. People had been looking for a good reason to downgrade the importance of winning anyway. Gallwey's book told them what they wanted to hear—that winning didn't matter—and its sales took off.

The only problem was that, try as they might to say it wasn't so, people still wanted to win, and deep down everybody knows it. It is like the old story where the dad comes home from his golf game and is greeted by his son who asks, "Did you win, Daddy?" And the father replies, "Charlie and I only play for fun. We are not really trying to win." "Okay then, Dad," his son continues, "Who had the most fun?"

Although it is helpful, when playing tennis or any other sport, to avoid consciously dwelling on winning during the course of competition, this is a far cry from saying winning doesn't matter. (Top athletes avoid thinking about winning during play by focusing narrowly on their game plans and small, helpful, mechanical aspects of their sport—effective because only one thought can occupy a person's mind at one time. In tennis, for example, this might involve filling one's mind with watching the ball, relaxing, and throwing one's weight into the shot. At the same time, however, great athletes darn well understand, at some basic mental level, that they want to win.) Gallwey's book notwithstanding, self-perceptive people simply know that they are happier and more satisfied when they win and are successful. People who lie to themselves by claiming that they don't care about winning simply end up losing more often than they should. The problems of competing successfully can certainly be solved, but first the issue of wanting to win, with its attendant fears, must be acknowledged and squarely faced.

WHERE DOES THE DRIVE TO COMPETE AND WIN COME FROM?

Oddly enough, the best explanation seems to come from animal studies. (See Appendix 2 for other explanations.) The work of Nobel prize-winning ethologist, Konrad Lorenz, who spent a lifetime studying the natural behavior of animals, provides fascinating insights into human nature by comparing our behavior to other species. We do lots of things that we think are uniquely human. Closer inspection, however, uncovers almost exact counterparts among the animal kingdom and suggests that these behaviors are, at least partially, genetically determined.

Lorenz studied aggression. He was interested in fighting between members of the same species, and though this might not, on the surface, seem directly applicable to competition between humans in sports or jobs, deeper analysis shows that it is. Animals compete by fighting and being aggressive for the things that are important to their lives, like mates, territory, food, and social position. They can't talk; they don't have money; there are no laws and policemen; and symbolism is meaningless to them, so fighting or threatening to fight is the only way they can enforce their wills on their fellows and take the things they want. The winner of the fight obtains the good things of life (at least as far as an animal is concerned), and the loser goes without.

Human beings are also after the good things in life and getting them often requires competing with and besting other people. In our case, because we are more complex creatures and symbolic battles can replace direct physical ones, we fight in more subtle ways. But at the deepest level, competition among humans has much in common with aggression or fighting in animals.

PEOPLE CAN'T RESIST TRYING TO BEST EACH OTHER

Human beings seem to have an endless desire to wage contests against each other. This is not just in sports, but occurs in every sphere of life. These contests sometimes engender elements of overt aggression and antagonism in which we have the urge to fight and defeat our fellows, either physically or symbolically. This happens in boxing and tennis. In other situations, such as, for example, golf or a race, where the contestants work separately against a clock rather than directly against each other, the competition is indirect and elicits less personal antagonism. This is also the case in business. It still involves competition, but the opponents are generally not face to face. But like overt fights, there are still winners and losers, and the core motivation is, in many ways, the same.

Of course, we experience periods of quiet where our softer sides predominate. We love our families, enjoy walks in the park, do charity work, have cohesive social instincts, and are obviously capable of loving and caring for each other. If one of our fellows is in danger, many of us will take substantial personal risks to save him. Yet there is also a darker side to our natures—that of aggression and competition. Whether we admit it or not, we would all like to elevate ourselves with respect to our fellows, and this involves, on some level, competition and often conflict. Our genes simply program us this way, and though we may be able to understand, tame, and control the beast, we will ultimately have to live with it.

ALL SPECIES FIGHT THEIR OWN KIND

Fighting one's own kind is common throughout the animal kingdom. In fact, every species that is capable of fighting does it, and they fight with whatever weapons they have. Animals with teeth bite, animals with claws scratch, those with horns butt, fish ram and bite each other, and frogs even jump and land on their opponent's back. The only species that don't attack each other are those that are physically incapable of doing so. For example, creatures like clams or earthworms simply have no weapons with which to fight.

The type of aggression that we are discussing is not directed at other species. There is some fighting of this kind, but it is the exception rather than the rule. Most fighting occurs when one member of a species fights another member of the same species. A lion attacking a zebra is not aggression; it is hunger—more like a human engaging a turkey at the dinner table as contrasted with two humans in a fistfight. Most prey animals will fight a predator if they are cornered and unable to flee, but this is relatively uncommon compared to the fights prey animals have with each other. In fact, the large antlers of the stag are used primarily for fights against rivals, whereas they generally defend themselves from predators by lashing out with their legs.

Lorenz studied interspecies and intraspecies fighting by putting 100 tropical fish in an aquarium and observing them. The 100 fish consisted of 25 different species with an average of four members of each species. He counted incidents of biting and found that the fish attacked their own kind six times as often as they attacked members of other species. This is interesting because in the aquarium each fish associates with 96 members of other species and only three members of his own. Somehow the fish manage to wend their ways peacefully through hordes of other species in order to seek out and attack the few members of their own kind.

THE AWFUL TRUTH ABOUT COMPETITION

Many of the characteristics of our animal brethren that we find so charming and attractive are really manifestations of their dark sides, their aggressive natures. For example, the lovely birdcalls we hear in the woods are not what poets have portrayed them to be—celebrations of their feelings of gladness and joy at the beauty of the day. Rather these calls are usually warnings to other males of the same species that a particular territory is occupied and they can expect a nasty fight if they enter. The characteristic and handsome red breast of the robin is a powerful stimulus to aggression in other male robins. And the distinctive bright color patterns of fish that inhabit coral reefs do not serve merely to dress up our aquariums. These aggressive little fish warn their fellow fish away with these colors. They need to recognize each other quickly at a distance lest they wander into occupied territory and get into a vicious scrap.

WHY DO ANIMALS BEHAVE THIS WAY?

What possible biological advantage could such behavior provide? After all, you would think that the animals would have enough to worry about escaping predators or chasing prey without fighting each other. The fact is that they are aggressive towards their own kind for many of the same reasons that we are: territory, mates, and position on the social hierarchy. In this way, the strongest, cleverest, and most dominant individuals are able to lead the social group, produce the most offspring, and have the wherewithal to feed and raise their young. It improves the species. The ones that are successful in fights with their fellows have a better chance of passing on their strong genes to the next generation. Aggressive instincts may not serve these biological purposes in human beings today because they evolved in a primitive world that no longer exists. Thirty thousand years ago there was no unemployment insurance to sustain those who were too weak or inept to obtain food. Their survival was at risk. Natural selection was free to produce beings that were aggressive and strong enough to take and hold the necessities of life. The weak had no choice but to take whatever was left and, therefore, fewer of their genes would have reached future generations. Though the world may have substantially changed since then, the aggressive instincts that allowed us to successfully compete against our fellows and produce large numbers of offspring remain.

THE DRIVE TO POSSESS TERRITORY

At first glance it would seem that the motives of the athlete or businessman are totally dissimilar from those of a male lion biting and clawing an interloping male on the African veldt. Yet they are very much the same. Consider territory, over which many animals are willing to fight. The males (for it is the male of the species that does most, though not by any means all, of the fighting in the animal kingdom) jealously guard a piece of ground and rush toward interloping males to attack and drive them to flight or submission. Why? Because for them it is the only possession worth holding onto. It is a larder where they can obtain food, it is stage where they can court females and demonstrate to them their prowess as a provider, and it is a refuge where they can raise their young. Unlike humans, animals don't have bank accounts, homes in the suburbs, stylish clothes, or flashy cars with which they can meet their material needs or impress ladies. Territory is the animal's only tangible source of security.

Individuals of their own kind are rivals for this territory because they fill the same ecological niche. On a coral reef, for example, there is an enormous variety of different species living harmoniously in close proximity to each other. They pose no threat to each other because they have different "occupations" and are not, therefore, in competition for limited food resources. Each species is a specialist in a particular manner of obtaining nutrients. Some eat other fish; some eat the coral itself; some can crack the hard shells of crabs and sea urchins to feast on the flesh within; others eat only marine plants, and so on. These fish have no reason to fight each other. They can "do business" right next to each other without quarrel because the food gathering of one has no effect on the food supply of the other. But the fish of the same species depend on the same food supply and would soon exhaust it if too many participants were congregated in a limited area. Aggression forces them to spread out. Territorial fish of the same species are genetically programmed to drive each other away in order to gain possession of and hold a small part of the coral reef for themselves.

HUMAN BEINGS ALSO LUST AFTER TERRITORY

In human beings, "territory" may take the form of a piece of ground, but it can also include other possessions as well. In our case, "territory" can be simply thought of as "things" which we feel belong to us, that we deem to be rightfully ours. These could be tangible like land, houses, furniture, cars, and money, or intangible like lines of credit or position at an intersection. Our proprietary feelings make us want to fight someone who tries to take them away or make unauthorized use of them. The interloper calls forth the urge to attack and safeguard what is ours. And this is not just a logical response in order that we may keep some valued possession. It is a deep and instantaneous emotional reaction. Our anger has feelings of indignation and legitimacy associated with it. Our urges to fight feel like righteous urges to take on the "good" fight.

In order to better understand the emotions associated with territorial defense, imagine walking into the living room of your home and finding an uninvited stranger pawing through your belongings. Your reaction would be instantaneous and electric. Anger and fear would surge through your emotional system, stress hormones would flow, and you would be physically and mentally prepared to fight the intruder. You might wisely choose not to do it, but you would certainly be on the emotional verge of doing so.

Now picture your feelings if an uninvited bird, dog, or cat were in your home rather than a human being. This would not be terribly troubling emotionally because creatures of other species do not threaten to take your property away. They might be a nuisance and dirty your floor, but they are not rivals for the possessions you value. A human being is another story. He is encroaching on your territory, and this engenders moral indignation and the urge to attack. In fact, you would feel pretty much like the coral fish does when a rival swims into his personal area of the reef.

Like the coral fish, Andy Roddick, Pete Sampras, John McEnroe, Henry Ford, John Rockefeller, and Bill Gates also aggressively competed for "territory" in its broadest sense. By defeating their fellows on their chosen battlefields, they won money and possessions. They were aggressive, acquisitive, and relentless. They were never content and tried to take as much territory as they could. They wanted it all and were prepared to leave nothing for anybody else. They did not "want," ultimately, to satisfy physical needs, but rather they simply and unceasingly "wanted." This insatiable greed for "more" is, in itself, interesting. It would fit well into Darwin's evolutionary theories because, harsh as it might seem, it would genetically benefit the human race. It would improve human genetics in two ways. First, the strong and clever (the "winners") would acquire massive amounts of territory with which to sustain a multitude of offspring, and second, the weak and slow (the "losers") would have all their territory taken away and be unable to sustain any offspring.

Genghis Khan, who conquered two-thirds of the known world in the thirteenth century, supplies the ultimate example of how this works. He was known to be sexually prolific on a massive scale. Accounts produced shortly after his death estimated his offspring and descendents at over 20,000. Incredibly, experts estimate that in the area of the world originally under his control, as much as eight percent of today's population retains some portion of his genetic material.

SUCCESS LEADS TO SEX

A second motivation for competition and aggression in the animal kingdom is sexual. Because males can generally impregnate multiple females and females must invest a greater proportion of their personal resources and energies in nurturing a particular brood of offspring, female receptivity is usually the limiting factor in mating. In general, the females choose from among competing males, and this competition assumes various forms whereby males sort themselves according to genetic suitability. The female's need is to acquire the best genes she can and, in some cases, adequate aid in nurturing and protecting the new family.

One such sorting mechanism involves physical battles between competing males. Sometimes the males are polygamous and manage to accumulate large harems. Not only do these successful competitors attract and hold the most desirable females, but they are also downright piggish about it and sometimes collect them all, leaving their unsuccessful rivals to go entirely without. Territory and sex often go together, attracting females being a major motivation for male animals to defeat rivals and dominate a territory. For the benefit of the species, most females are genetically programmed to be attracted to the winners and possessors of property.

There are parallels in human behavior, although there are substantial differences as well. With human beings, both men and women are, in general, attracted to members of the opposite sex who are competent and successful, but there are differences in degree. In general, men are more attracted by physical appearance and women by competence and success. Of course, both are attracted by appearance as well as competence, but they each give these factors different weights. Because of this, there are differences in the reasons why males and females compete and strive for success. Men do it, partially, to become more sexually attractive to women. (As Andy Roddick once quipped after being tabbed by the media as one of the sexiest men in the world, "Funny, the more I win, the sexier I get!" Women, in contrast, are not obliged to compete for this reason. Rather, they do it for the personal and social reasons which we will discuss in greater detail later in this chapter.

Most men understand, at some level, that women will be more attracted to them if they are successful and powerful—if they have managed to take and hold "territory." Walk the streets of wealthy communities like Beverly Hills and Brentwood and notice the women in and around the fancy shops and restaurants. A disproportionate number are very pretty. Note the looks of women driving late model expensive cars like Mercedes Benz, Lexus, BMW, and Jaguar. You will also see an abnormally high percentage of pretty ladies. Why? Because a great many women gravitate toward competent, successful men, and most men gravitate toward pretty women.

And many of these women are not simply enamored with the expensive possessions that wealthy men can provide. They are often attracted by his capacity for success itself—the man's personal power and ability to win. (Of course it often goes the other way too, but not to the same degree.) Young, pretty women who marry older, wealthy men do not, in many cases, do it for the money in the simple sense that elicits snide remarks and knowing smiles. They are often equally attracted by the man's competence. The outside world can be harsh and threatening, and a man with proven ability to achieve and succeed can provide a degree of comfort and protection. This is not in any way to deny the fact that many powerful women are dynamic achievers in their own right and can get along quite well on their own. Society has changed in recent years, and women have begun to make a substantial impact in the workplace. But even these women yearn for competent men who have abilities commensurate

24

with their own. With men, on the other hand, this requirement can be frequently overpowered by a curvaceous shape, shimmering hair, a pretty face, and friendly manner.

WINNING MAKES US SEXUAL

Not only is male competitive success an aphrodisiac to many females, but it also heightens the sex drives of the victorious males, while losing has the opposite effect. For example, if a male buck loses his territory in a rival fight and is, in a sense, paupered, he also loses interest in sex and will not mate, even when a willing female is available. Of course, we have no way of knowing what emotions this situation really evokes, but the losing buck acts as if he feels weakened, disgraced, unconfident, and too demoralized to perform sexually. For awhile, losing this contest functionally emasculates him. By the same token, it is common for human males who suffer business setbacks, thereby losing "territory," to become depressed and, like the buck, lose interest in sex. (Harvard anthropologist Richard Wrangham provides a possible physiological explanation. Before athletic contests or fights, male testosterone levels—which correlate positively with sexuality as well as aggressive behavior—tend to rise. After the contest, the winning male's testosterone level remains elevated, while the losers' generally drops. Moreover, this phenomenon even occurs in intellectual contests like chess and trivia games.)

In contrast, powerful, successful men may have greater sexual appetites than ordinary men—a theory supported by a great deal of anecdotal evidence as well as analogy with other species. Darwin and natural selection would have predicted that the species would be best served if successful males were genetically inclined and able to mate more frequently than unsuccessful males. Consistent with this hypothesis is the finding that "hyperthermic" men have high sexual appetites as well as upbeat, optimistic, energetic, and decisive personalities—traits that predispose them to be successful in business, sports, politics, and other competitive arenas. Furthermore, high testosterone level in males is associated with high sexuality as well as dominance and high aggression.

Documented cases of sexual excess involving men in high places are extraordinarily frequent, sometimes in the face of great risk. John Kennedy, Ted Kennedy, Gary Hart, Bob Packwood, and Bill Clinton are recent standouts in the political realm. But almost to the man, the presidents of the United States have been discovered in adulterous, illicit affairs, the public exposure of which could have seriously damaged their careers. Yet they were so sexually driven that they were willing to accept this risk. Victor Hugo's need and capability to have sex nine times a day was described in Graham Robb's biography, and Julius Caesar's sexual appetite was legendary in ancient times. As described by philosopher Will Durant in his book *Caesar and Christ*, Caesar had sexual relationships with "Cleopatra of Egypt, with Queen Eunoe in Numidia, and with so many ladies in Gaul that his soldiers in fond jest called him mocus calvus, 'the bald adulterer;' in his triumph after conquering Gaul they sang a couplet warning all husbands to keep their wives under lock and key as long as Caesar was in town." Pompey, Caesar's greatest rival, divorced his wife for intimacy with Caesar, and Cato, his most vociferous enemy in the Senate, carried a personal grudge because his sister, Servilia, was the most devoted of Caesar's mistresses. (The causal link between success and sexual appetite is hard to prove on the basis of anecdotal evidence because successful men are more attractive to women than are other men, so their plethora of sexual encounters may be as much a function of opportunity as appetite.)

I WAS NOT IMMUNE

In any case, it is clear that in males sex is a powerful motive for competition, achievement, and success. Males certainly understand, at some level, that their attractiveness to ladies is heavily influenced by successful achievement. We suspect that as much as women might find male sensitivity endearing, they still don't like losers. When I was young and competing in tennis tournaments, I remember well how sex pervaded my thoughts and how intimately it was involved in my drive for success. I used to think, not without justification, that winning tournaments would make the girls like me better. Tennis stars like Pete Sampras, John McEnroe, and Andre Agassi have never had great difficulty attracting beautiful women, and I suspect that Bill Gates could have done pretty well too on the single's scene. If, on the other hand, they had all been box-boys at the local supermarket and reliant only on their looks for dates, they might have found the going a little tougher.

Studies among high school students have shown that the most important factor in a boy's popularity with girls is competitive success in sports. (Later on, of course, money becomes a little more interesting.) With girls, on the other hand, popularity in high school is determined primarily by the "ability to get along" with others and "looks." Athletic success ranks lower, so women do not have the same motivations for competing in sports as do men. This does not necessarily mean that women are less competitive, just that their reasons for competing are different. Attractiveness to the opposite sex is not nearly as high on the women's list of reasons for wanting to win as it is on the men's.

For men in the business world, the trappings of financial success are important, at least in part, because of their attraction to the ladies. Businessmen know that an expensive car, elegant home, and powerful corporate position will make him attractive to women in the same way as tournament victories and headlines do for the professional athlete. When I was in the investment business and driving a Porsche, I recall going out on a first date when my car was in the shop for repairs, and I was driving a rattletrap loaner. As I walked my date from her house to my car, I had the distinct feeling that I was sinking in her esteem. I hate to admit this, because it does smack of having a character weakness, but I would have liked to have declared that this crummy car was in no way representative of me or my achievement abilities—that I had a better one, and this was just a loaner. I simply did not want to start off a leg down by looking like someone who was having trouble making money in business.

WE ALL WANT TO BE AT THE TOP OF THE HEAP

The third major motive for competition and aggression among social species is to elevate one's position in the group's social hierarchy. We all have a social ranking of sorts and success in competition has placed Andre Agassi, Serena Williams, Sheri Lansing (CEO of Paramount Studios), and Bill Gates above most of us. All social animals have a ranking order such that all the individuals in the society know which other individuals are stronger or weaker than they are. Each gives way to the stronger while expecting submission from the weaker. Known amongst domestic fowl as "pecking order," this expression has been applied to animals that do not peck but rather bite or clash horns. As originally conceived, the term meant that the most powerful bird had the right to peck all the other birds while they dared not peck it. The second most powerful could peck all the birds weaker than it but had to submit to pecking from the top bird, and so on down to the bottom bird who could get pecked by all the other birds but could not peck anyone itself.

SOCIAL INSTINCTS HAVE SURVIVAL VALUE

Social species like human beings, wolves, and chimpanzees have unique advantages over solitary species. Wolf packs can drag down and kill animals that are too large and powerful to tackle alone. Moreover, they can avoid serious injury, which is generally fatal in the wild, by threatening a dangerous prey from several directions at once and allowing some of their members to attack a vulnerable flank. Using "mobbing" techniques, large groups of prey animals sometimes drive off predators and save themselves. Temporarily disabled individuals can be fed and protected by the group until they heal. And human

27

beings have achieved unchallenged planetary supremacy by pooling resources and working in groups, while alone, survival itself would have been doubtful.

And because human social instincts were, in prehistoric times, so important for individual survival, it is reasonable to assume that they are deeply imbedded in our genetic codes. We are programmed to care about what other people think of us. Those early individuals who did not care would have risked being ejected from the group—a virtual death sentence in those days. Alone and with little chance of survival, their genes would have been removed from the human gene pool. Thus the people that remained would be genetically driven to worry about what other people thought of them. Today, virtually all of us, at some deep, primitive level, long for positive acclaim from other people.

That is why certain "old saws" that our parents fed to us when we were children are so totally flawed. Our parents tried to shield us from hurt by telling us that being teased, called names, or belittled by our classmates should not bother us. "Who cares what they say?" our parents would declare. After all, "Sticks and stones can break your bones, but words can never harm you."

Nothing could be further from the truth. In fact, the exact opposite is the case. Because of our social instincts, words, insults, or public disgrace remain painful long after the effects of any physical hurt dissipate. Most of us can eventually forgive and forget a blow but find it difficult, if not impossible, to ever get over an insult.

DIFFERENT TEMPERMENTS ARE USEFUL

In order for social creatures to reap communal benefits, it is imperative that the individuals in the group have different capabilities and temperaments. The social group would not function well if its members were all born the same because the many different functions in a complex society require different capabilities, though this concept seems to distress some philosophers, psychologists, and proponents of certain social agendas. The group requires a social hierarchy and chain of command with acknowledged leaders and followers. Everybody must understand his relative social position in order to reduce conflicts and allow the group to work together efficiently. Nature and genetics have addressed this by designing the individual members of social species to vary in personality and aptitude.

For example, the members of a wolf pack are all different. Some are aggressive, others passive; some are inquisitive and want to explore, others are content to remain near the familiar; some are courageous fighters, while others shrink from danger. But together they form a cohesive, effective pack of hunters and they all survive. The dominant, aggressive ones lead, and the others follow. If they were all dominant and aggressive, there would be constant and ruinous fighting for position. By themselves, the timid, accommodating ones might not survive, but within the pack, they function well and provide necessary "glue" to hold the pack together. Each wolf has a different role to play during the hunt and while living as part of the group, and it is essential they each have different temperaments and capabilities.

In contrast, solitary creatures are all very much the same. This suits them because each individual must perform all the functions necessary for its survival. It cannot depend on others of its kind to supply assets that it may lack. Red foxes, for example, are solitary hunters, not social animals, and the temperament of each kit in the litter is the same—aggressive, inquisitive, playful, and courageous. They have to be this way to survive. Natural selection took care of this through the evolutionary process. Any kit that lacked these characteristics simply did not survive, and its genes, therefore, died out.

WE ALL HUNGER FOR HIGH STATUS

Social creatures that we are, human beings are powerfully driven to test our upper social limits and rise as high as possible on the social hierarchy. As human beings, we differ in aggressiveness and competitiveness, although we are all aggressive and competitive to some extent, and we all innately strive, within the limits imposed by our temperaments, capabilities, and experiences, to rise to our highest possible social positions. We all push to elevate ourselves above our fellows, or at least to resist having our fellows elevate themselves above us. We are terribly concerned with status. Since this status, as with all social creatures, is largely determined by our success in competition, we are forcefully driven to compete.

This status-seeking behavior obviously has a genetic basis because it occurs in so many different cultures separated by such great distances. Europeans look up to the owners of expensive luxury cars just as do Americans or Japanese. Gold Rolex watches or the latest fashions in clothing make their owners feel important, whether they live in New York, Rome, Tel Aviv, Jakarta, Nairobi, Lima, or New Delhi. It is terribly unlikely that parents so disparate in culture and so widely distant would all happen to teach their children to seek status. And even if the parents did teach children to seek status, the next question would be, "Why did all these parents, who come from such different cultures

29

and geographical areas, happen to teach their children these things?" If genetics did not underlie these teachings, parents would have taught their children differently.

THE GOVERNMENT CAN'T DRIVE IT OUT OF US

The Soviets found this out during the seventy years of their communist system when they tried to impose their ideas of personal equality and communality on the people. The government used propaganda and coercion, but it never worked. Like a stretched spring, as soon as the pressure for conformity was released, the people popped back to competing for status.

I played in the Soviet National tennis championship in Moscow in 1965 and had a chance to watch their system in action. Since the production of clothing was controlled by the government, there was virtually no fashion industry. For example, they had one type of raincoat that came in several colors. It was not bad looking, but it was the only one you could get, and walking down a Moscow street on a rainy day, it was striking to see everyone wearing the same brand of raincoat. Try as they might, however, the Russian government could not teach their people to enjoy dressing alike and to forgo their desires for the latest American jeans or fashions.

As a foreign tennis player, I had a couple of suitcases full of stylish clothing, and I soon found out that the tremendous demand for these items in Russia gave rise to a flourishing black market. Shirts that cost $10 in the USA would fetch more than 30 rubles in Moscow (the exchange rate was 1 ruble = $1.10 at the time). The Russians certainly had adequate clothing, but they wanted "fashionable" clothing—clothing that everyone else didn't have. Tennis was an amateur game at the time so I was not averse to picking up some extra income by selling shirts. (But the Russians had the last laugh. After I got the rubles, I learned that there was nothing worth having that you could buy with them.)

THE OBJECT IS TO GET ON TOP

Status is, of course, relative, not absolute, so there is an element of getting ahead of others involved in raising one's status. In the poorest African country, for example, the man with a few cattle is elevated over the man without any, and the man with a beat-up automobile might have higher status than either of them. Status is determined by one's ability, in some measurable way, to rise above the other members of one's group, neighborhood, or tribe. People living in poorer American neighborhoods only feel underprivileged because their living standards compare unfavorably with Beverly Hills. If they had that same house in a small village in Pakistan, they would feel like kings.

WHERE DOES JEALOUSY COME FROM?

My own personal experience with competition has shown me that the genetic drives are powerful enough to thwart years of counter-training. My mother was a very loving person—unselfish to an extreme, strongly religious, and a student of Eastern philosophy. Her heroes were Mahatma Ghandi and Albert Schweitzer; she believed in the basic goodness of man; and she was concerned with the welfare of everyone she met. (I must have taken after my father.) My earliest recollection is of her telling me that helping others is mankind's highest goal and that self-love is secondary to the love for others.

So why was it that when I was playing in the number two position on the UCLA tennis team behind my best friend, Larry Nagler, I secretly wanted him to lose so I could play ahead of him? Who taught me the feeling of jealousy? Who teaches it to everyone? Why do we want to see the mighty fall and our friends be less successful than we are? I was certainly not taught to think that way, in fact quite the contrary. The answer is that feelings of jealousy are genetic. They are simply manifestations of our drive to elevate our positions in the social hierarchy by lowering the status of those that are above us.

Certain aspects of crowd psychology are also motivated by jealousy. Why do crowds naturally pull for underdogs? Who bothers to teach them this? Obviously, no one. Most people are not good at winning, so they identify with the underdogs. The underdogs are like them, so they want to see them drag the favorites down, to lower the favorites' statuses and bring them more into line with their own. Similarly, the reading public that frequent trashy publications like the *Enquirer*, *Globe*, *Examiner*, and *Star*, eagerly feast upon the drug problems, diseases, divorces, infidelities, and other foibles of the famous. The readers feel better about their own positions when they learn that the stars are not doing so well after all. The Germans even have a word for it, "schadenfreude," which translates to "happiness in other people's misery." (See Appendix 3 for how status effects social interactions on the professional tennis circuit.)

THE NEED FOR FULFILLMENT

"Are there no higher, more uplifting factors that propel achievement beyond our rather grubby and animalistic lustings after sex, territory, and position?" you may rightfully ask. Yes, there are. The humanist psychologists like Maslow,

Rogers, and White theorized that we are also driven to use our potentialities and to self-actualize. These are our higher urges. We seek competence. We strive to create. In essence, their theories propose that we are driven to use all the capabilities we may have—i.e., that along with the gift of these capabilities, nature gives us the drive to use them. For example, a baby is driven to move its body, vocalize, or explore its environment simply because it is able to do so. Similarly, we may compete in sports for the simple joy of competing; we may run and exercise for the pleasure of using our bodies; we may enjoy creating because we are endowed with creative abilities.

This fulfillment theory adds an additional dimension to achievement beyond the practical and social needs previously discussed. Though the need for fulfillment is secondary to these other needs, it explains why a person might paint a beautiful picture that no one else will ever see. It is why we might sing in the shower or enjoy beautiful scenery. It is the reason someone might delight in playing a musical instrument well without an audience. It provides an alternative reason as to why people might continue to work and build up their businesses when they no longer need money—because they feel they are creating something with lasting significance. It is the reason I am writing this book.

THE RELATIONSHIP BETWEEN CREATIVITY AND PERMANENCE

To me, this book represents something of value that I can leave behind. It will be here when I no longer am and, therefore, enhances my pursuit of permanence. Most of us, at some level of consciousness, recognize the insignificance and short span of our existences. We try to compensate by seeking permanence in any way we can. I did it, in my younger years, by winning tennis tournaments. My name was inscribed in the permanent records alongside the champions of the past and would remain to be joined by the champions of the future. It gave my victories a feeling of substance. Many of us look for permanence in our children. We give birth to them, help them grow, teach them, and they go forth as our creative contribution to humanity's future. We derive a feeling of continuity. We obtain some of these same feelings by helping or teaching young people. Architects build buildings for the same reasons. Religion fulfills many of these needs as well. As believers, we become part of something more grand, powerful, and, most importantly, more lasting than our own miniscule, temporary existences. The list could continue, but I'll stop here.

Whether our drive for achievement is motivated by our creative or our more animalistic urges, we are all happier if, with the passage of time, we are getting better at something. Human beings are, in a broad sense, "project oriented" and derive satisfaction from progressing upward in almost any realm. For example, my happiest days as a tennis player were when I was getting better. It became less pleasant when I stopped improving and downright unpleasant when I started getting worse. We derive feelings of satisfaction as our bank accounts increase, our businesses get better, we improve our golf, our children grow, we learn to play an instrument, etc. A portion of this satisfaction results from the improvement itself, independent even of any practical consequences. And that is why successful achievement of any kind is so valuable.

In contrast, we become dissatisfied when improvement stops—when our lives plateau or decline. That is why so many people become restless and even depressed when their children leave home or when they retire from their jobs. They lack direction or a project upon which to focus their energies and needs for improvement. Aimless lives are often unhappy lives. (Food for thought: Might not these urges supply unconscious, underlying motivation for much of the terrorism that plagues the world today? Lacking constructive projects upon which to focus their urges to build and create, many people, particularly those in failed societies, are ripe for indoctrination into destructive ones. Feeling the need to do something important, something worthwhile, these deluded individuals may be able to morph normally constructive urges into diabolical destructive plots. Religious fanaticism and distain for Western society merely supply cover for jealousy and other evil impulses that they dare not admit, even to themselves.)

So far we have explored the power and pervasiveness of our genetic drives to achieve, compete, and win. But as we shall see in the next chapter, we are also taught to compete and succeed. Our parents and society as a whole push us to do so also.

HOW SOCIETY PRESSURES US TO WIN

Our desire to win and become successful is influenced by environmental factors— especially social and parental pressures.

NATURE VS. NURTURE

The distinction between genetic and learned drives is an important one. Obviously, most of our motives are combinations of both, but to really understand ourselves, we must carefully distinguish between them. (There are a third set of drives that are learned but "imprinted" at a crucial early age and, in later life, resemble genetic drives.) The genetic ones are always there, no matter what we are taught and no matter how often we are told it is wrong to have them. Not understanding this is a constant source of conflict and guilt. Learning can change our behavior, but it cannot remove underlying genetic drives. Jealousy and aggression, since they are genetic, will not go away, no matter how desperately we might wish they would. However, they can be controlled. It is, in a sense, like walking down the street and having the urge to urinate. Our instinct is to stop and do it right on the spot. We don't, of course, because we learn it is socially unacceptable, so we continue walking until we find a lavatory. Our underlying urge has not gone away. Only our behavior has been modified to conform to social norms. And for the purposes of society, that is good enough.

BEWARE OF PSYCHOLOGISTS

Thus far I have been putting heavy emphasis on the genetic factors driving us to compete and want to win. This does not mean that environmental factors are unimportant. Learning, too, is a significant part of the equation. But I have an instinctive negative reaction to the overemphasis on learned drives that has pervaded psychological thought in the last half century. In the 1920s John Watson founded the behaviorist school of psychology and declared, to enthusiastic audiences, that human instincts were virtually nonexistent. He believed that we were, at birth, like blank pieces of paper, ready to be completely molded by experience and conditioning. Watson thought that babies were endlessly malleable and adaptable and that, in the hands of a competent psychologist (one who used the latest conditioning techniques), anybody could learn to perform any job and develop any desired personality.

Ridiculous as these ideas might be, psychologists loved them for several reasons. First, it made psychologists more important. They could control conditioning and learning but were powerless to change genetics. It was not unpleasant for them to hear Watson say that genetics were irrelevant. Second, there is a whiff of bigotry and political incorrectness in the genetic emphasis. It is vaguely elitist and antidemocratic to accept that people may be born with widely different abilities and temperaments, that these differences are genetically determined, and that everyone is not capable of performing any job or rising to any height. Political liberalism has been, for many years, the zeitgeist in psychological academic circles, and it has exerted subtle pressure to magnify the importance of learning and downplay the role of genetics. The layman might like to believe that science strictly seeks the truth and that political correctness does not influence scientific thought. Unfortunately, this is not the case. Not only does science respond to the political climate currently in vogue (especially if the scientists want to get their paws on hefty government research grants), but there is also a "herd" mentality in research. Recent advances in genetic research have started the pendulum swinging back.

THE PRESSURE TO WIN

It is clear that both learning and genetics play important roles in our development, though which of the two is more powerful, no one can yet say with certainty. (Although my money is on genetics.) Whatever our natures might be, Western culture strongly conditions us to be competitive. There is tremendous social pressure to be successful. We are brought up amidst all manner of score-keeping devices which distinguish between winners and losers. Sport is an obvious example. As children, when we win our Little League games, people congratulate us and appear happy about our success. When we lose, they console us. Young though we might be, the message is clear—"Winning is better than losing." We are ranked according to school grades. When we come home sporting an "A," we get a much warmer reception than with a "C." Even the most politically correct and liberal parents—parents who firmly believe in the latest dubious self-esteem theories and who would never castigate or punish children for poor grades—even these parents cannot help being more joyous with high grades than mediocre ones. Kids can read between the lines; there is pressure to win.

And the pressure does not end when we reach adulthood. People treat successful and unsuccessful people differently. For example, when a group of business people gathers to discuss the events of the day, whose words have the most weight? The one with the most money! Most people would listen to the opinions of Bill Gates or Warren Buffett on anything before they would listen to the owner of the local gas station. By the same token, the tennis "stars" are more important and respected in the group than the "also-rans," and people are more apt to listen to what they say. Who would not be more attentive to Andy Roddick, Andre Agassi, or Serena Williams than they are to the player ranked 100? It is the same in all fields. In a group of scientists, the opinions of a Nobel Prize winner get more consideration than those of the average Ph.D. Even if we were not driven to compete and succeed at birth, our parents, associates, and society give us every incentive to become that way over time.

OUR PARENTS MAKE US DO IT

Family upbringing has a particularly important effect on this drive for success, termed by some psychologists as "need for achievement" and defined as "the desire to reach a standard of excellence in order to gain reward." Although there is undoubtedly a genetic component to this drive, early life experience has been shown to play a major role in its development. Moreover, "need for achievement" can be measured by tests, and studies have shown that children who receive high scores are likely to become successful competitors in all walks of life. They are the "pushers and shakers" who make things happen. They do well in school, sports, and business. They are the kind of people who can carry their whole society upward with them in their quest for success.

Studies involving the need for achievement have produced results that have interesting implications in the field of child development. Researchers have found that high achievers are produced by parents who expect their children to show an early independence and who set difficult standards for them. They reward their children for doing well with affection and are unhappy with failure.

37

MOM IS THE KEY

With boys, in particular, it has been shown that there is a dramatic difference depending on which parent does the pushing. In an oft-quoted study by Rosen and D'Andrade done in 1959, boys tested for achievement drive were divided into two groups based on their results—high and low achievers. They were brought into the laboratory and told to compete in a variety of tasks. Both parents were invited to be present and to participate. With the high-achieving boys, Rosen and D'Andrade noticed that the mothers took a forceful role "pushing, encouraging, rewarding, and punishing." The fathers meanwhile, seemed content to let the boys work on their own.

With the low achieving boys, the mothers stood back, while if anyone pushed, it tended to be a dominating father. Apparently, the concerned mother is able to impress her own standards on her son without great risk of backlash—interestingly, often rewarding him with physical affection. On the other hand, the domineering father seems to pose a threat and, in fact, can hold his son down if he becomes too forceful.

A study by University of Chicago education professor Benjamin Bloom involving 120 of the country's highest achieving athletes, artists, and scientists, backs up the idea that great success is more a product of upbringing than talent. In interviews he learned that few of these extraordinary people were child prodigies. Often a sibling appeared more naturally talented. But early parental influence was crucial. Bloom said, "These parents placed great stress on achievement, on success and doing one's best at all times. They were models of the 'work ethic,' believing that work should come before play and that one should always work toward distant goals."

The development of these extraordinary achievers generally went through three stages. In the first, the parents exposed their young children (five to nine years of age) to their sports, instruments, or science games in a fun manner. The parents or sometimes a neighbor or relative instructed them, they developed the habits of practice, and, sometime during the next three to five years, the kids began to get local recognition for their skills. The kids began to see themselves in terms of their chosen talent field.

In the second stage, the parents obtained more expert coaching for their children. Development was rapid—the coaches were perfectionists; practice times lengthened; and the kids worked diligently on technique. Here, as adolescents, the children began to experience very high-level results—winning state championships, doing independent research projects, or performing occasionally with symphony orchestras.

During the final stage, the subjects of the study began to "live" for their sports, instruments, etc. They devoted massive amounts of time for practice and sought out the best coaches and teachers in the country. At this stage, they reached world class and focused on developing personal styles and on the subtle refinements of their fields. Now they were internally driven and totally devoted to achieving higher goals.

Although they had to forego many of the normal "pleasures" of youth, few regretted their devotion to their fields. They stated that they felt better being productive than hanging out with friends and going to fast food restaurants. They were proud of their accomplishments, even after their days of glory had passed. Bloom concluded that many people have the ability to become extraordinary achievers if their embryonic talents are nurtured diligently, particularly by involved and thoughtful parents.

THE POWER OF THE JEWISH MOTHER

My own case is a good example. My father died when I was ten years old, and I was the apple of my mother's eye. She constantly pushed me to achieve, but at the same time she was affectionate and kind. She would say, "What have you done to better yourself today?" If I came home with a "B," she wanted to know why I didn't get an "A," because, she claimed, I was certainly capable of it. It seemed as though there was always more that could be done, and she was lavish with praise when I did it. She was the typical "Jewish Mother," and it seems quite possible that this remarkable species of womanhood has been largely responsible for the unusual degree of productivity and achievement of the Jewish people.

It is not, by any means, a proven fact that all boys should be pushed to achieve by their mothers and that their fathers should stay out of the way. There are plenty of cases where fathers have done great jobs motivating and guiding the developments of their sons. But the father must push his son more carefully than the mother. The son does not try to emulate his mother. She poses no threat to him, and he is unlikely to become overawed or frightened of her. When the mother pushes, the worst that can happen is that the son will consider her to be a nag. This is not the case with the father. A domineering, successful father can present a giant figure to a son, and he is capable of applying too much power for the son to handle. As a result, the son may shrink in the father's shadow rather than grow.

Although the evidence is not conclusive, the message appears to be that a loving, supportive mother who pushes her son to early independence and demands high standards can help produce a child with a high need for achievement. A father can also do this, but he must be more circumspect and careful in his approach. He can also set standards and goals but must take care to avoid being overbearing and domineering. (See Appendix 4 for the implications of single parenthood.)

RAISING A WINNING DAUGHTER

It is more difficult to make general statements about how the need for achievement develops in women because most of the research has been done on males. Since learning plays an important role in the need for achievement, culturally determined sex roles are important. Although our culture has changed in recent years, our society still pressures men to be aggressive, competitive and successful, and women to be supportive, get along with others, and be socially acceptable. In addition, genetic differences between the sexes direct them in a like manner.

On the other hand, the high divorce rate and breakdown of the family unit has thrust increasing numbers of women into the workplace where their dramatic successes have provided increasing numbers of powerful role models for their young sisters. No longer does our society expect women to be pigeonholed strictly into their traditional roles of wives and mothers. Yet our society is in a state of flux along these lines, and women oft times get contradictory and confusing messages. How are they to go about knocking heads, competing, and achieving while simultaneously remaining soft, feminine, and nurturing? How are they to walk the delicate tightrope between their familial responsibilities and their career goals? Pulling this off requires talents bordering on the mythical (in addition to being able to function well while sleep-deprived).

Women often bring certain talents to the world of business that can give them an advantage over their male counterparts. Among these are their verbal and people-skills. Since success in business almost always involves understanding what other people are up to and moving others to do what one wants, these skills are exceedingly valuable. During their formative years, young males spend a great deal of energy working to excel and beat people in sports and games. Most females, meanwhile, are honing their abilities to get along with people, to move them subtly, and to read the nuances of their facial expressions, gestures, and speech intonations. Young males (and many older ones as well) are often unaware that this world of social subtlety even exists and, in contrast, tend to employ forceful and direct means to get what they want—an approach that can often prove disadvantageous.

As for achievement drives, we know that parents who urge and expect their daughters to be productive and successful do create achievers. It is not known whether role reversal applies and females develop into achievers best when pushed by their fathers, but this hypothesis does possess a certain comforting symmetry.

Along this line, there is a great deal of anecdotal evidence that, at least with women tennis players, fathers can be particularly successful at pushing their daughters to become champions. In fact, the fathers of tennis stars Jennifer Capriati, Venus and Serena Williams, Jelena Dokic, and Mary Pierce have been accused in the press on multiple occasions of going too far in driving and controlling the careers of their daughters. In the case of Mary Pierce's father, there were stories of actual physical abuse. With some of the others, the paternal drive was just overly strong and occasionally borderline abusive. But in all cases, it was dominating and controlling in the extreme. Yet these young ladies were instilled with the intense drive to practice hour after hour and year after year in their successful quests to become the tennis champions for which their fathers hungered. Most people would term this level of parental pushing "dysfunctional," but the incredible level of drive required to play championship tennis is, in itself, somewhat "dysfunctional." (Average people do not want to practice anything for four hours a day for ten years. Only the intensely driven will do it.) In any case, dysfunctional or not, in many cases it seems to work.

On the other hand, this particular group of young ladies has also exhibited an unusual degree of emotional instability as competitors. For years the Williams sisters became inordinately nervous at crucial stages in big matches, claimed to be injured unusually often (leading skeptical fellow players to suspect hypochondria), and even talked about quitting the tour early to pursue other interests. (Because of their incredible athletic abilities and extraordinary drive, the sisters became world champions in spite of these problems.) Mary Pierce, a former French champion, has tailed off as a competitor. Her apathy in training and competition drove off several coaches, and by 2003, she has become overweight and only a sporadically successful competitor. Dokic is also reput-

41

ed to be an uncertain competitor, having reached the semifinal at Wimbledon in 1999 (after upsetting world number one ranking Martina Hingis in the first round) and following it up with a first round loss at the Australian Open. And Jennifer Capriati was off the tour for several years with a well-publicized bout of drug problems before managing to right herself and win the Australian Open in 2001. Since then, she has competed well but exhibited bouts of emotional instability, one of which led her, in 2002, to abuse Federation Cup captain, legendary Billie Jean King, and get kicked off the team.

All of which leads me to conclude that parents can certainly enhance competitive and achievement drives in their children, but in order to develop an emotionally stable child, the parental push should be temperate and balanced. Since the pathway to excellence, be it in sports, business, or the arts, is always difficult, often uphill, and strewn with sweat and even tears, parents should stress the relationship between hard work and success. (One can never repeat this too often or emphasize its importance too strongly.) In addition, a reasonable level of early parental "push" can often help children get "over the hump" in these endeavors so that the children become competent enough to enjoy working on further improvement themselves. Like jump-starting a car, you push until its own engine kicks in, and then it goes by itself. In my own case, my mother forced me to play tennis at first. I did not want to play. But after a few months, I got good enough to play my first local tournament, had some small success, and I was hooked. Thereafter, I was self-motivated to practice constantly.

IT'S NEVER TOO LATE

Even if you emerged from childhood with a low need for achievement, it may not be too late to develop it—provided that you feel such a drive is desirable. It does, after all, tend to increase one's level of stress and, therefore, may not be emotionally pleasant or physically healthy. On the other hand, this type of stress is hard to avoid in our society which places such a premium on success. Being a laid-back, nonachiever might be soothing and healthy in a setting where no one is keeping score, but here our associates keep us running to stay up. Most of us feel badly if we don't, no matter what we may tell ourselves.

Increasing one's need for achievement as an adult is possible, although scientific research on the subject is far from complete. Basically, it requires a change in one's thinking process—a reorganization of one's priorities. One needs to break down habitual thought patterns, placing greater importance on goals, so that certain aspects of life's continuing puzzle take on different values.

Tests were carried out on college students and businessmen where they were given specific achievement training. As a result, school grades improved and the businessmen began working longer hours and were more aggressive in getting new business, increasing their authority, and moving upward within their firms. How did they do it? Simply by getting together in groups for various periods of time to talk and think specifically about achievement. They were encouraged to discuss their fantasies about it, to set specific goals for themselves, and to act out roles and play games involving achievement. By doing this, they became accustomed to focusing on achievement, which caused them to rearrange their priorities and place achievement in a higher position than before.

In an informal way, business people do this when they gather in groups. They discuss the stock market, the economy, or their latest business deals. This increases their interest and drive for business success. And the tennis players on the pro circuit do the same thing. They sit around at the courts and talk endlessly about tennis—old matches, recent matches, strategy, analysis of each other's weaknesses and strengths. You name it, and, providing it has to do with winning tennis matches, they talk about it. It drives their wives crazy, but it does serve to involve the players ever deeper into the game, keeping their drive levels high.

So far we have been discussing the drive to win and to achieve—its origin and deep pervasiveness. But if it is such a powerful drive, why is it apparently lacking in so many individuals? Why are so few people excellent competitors? As we shall see in the following chapters, it is because wanting to win is only part of the story.

THE INSIDIOUS AND PERVASIVE FEAR OF FAILURE

All competition and drives for achievement are accompanied by a fear of failure, which must be controlled in order to succeed.

O ur drives to win, achieve, and succeed are not, unfortunately, able to function unencumbered. Fear of failure lurks in the background, threatening at any time to rise up and debilitate us. Though it may sometimes be motivating, this fear is usually destructive of achievement, occasionally, overwhelmingly so.

PEOPLE ARE BESET WITH GENERALIZED INSECURITIES AND FEARS

First, let us examine generalized fear, which may or may not directly impact our abilities to compete effectively. Famed psychologist Alfred Adler, a member of Freud's inner circle, sensed the importance of generalized fears when he proposed that man's drive for power stemmed from his need to compensate for deep feelings of insecurity and inferiority. (The drive for power was as central to Adler's motivational theories as sex was to Freud's.) It was Adler who coined the phrase "inferiority complex" and theorized that we spend our lives struggling upward to achieve goals in order to convince ourselves that we are not, in fact, inferior, and to distance ourselves from our fears.

No one knows whether we are born with generalized feelings of insecurity and fear or whether we develop them early in life, but it is clear that such feelings are a common human condition. And there is little doubt that they impact, at least to some extent, our abilities to achieve and compete. Some people's lives are dominated by fears, others experience less, but even the strongest among us have occasional rushes of it where we sense our own miniscule importance and feel impotent in the face of the vast forces beyond our ken. The world is a complex place, and our minds are small. Worst of all, our lives are short. We are on the brink of the abyss, and our physical existences will soon end. Our every nerve ending has been programmed with the instinct for self-preservation—to resist, above all, the physical dissolution of death. Yet, we know it must come and that for all the eternity to follow we will cease to exist. I, for one, am not ashamed to admit that these thoughts scare the HELL out of me. My solution, like most people, is to simply not think about it. But of course we all know that it hasn't really gone away. Rather, vague fears skulk at the margins of consciousness—to surface occasionally when we are alone in the dark of night (or when our airplanes hit turbulence).

We struggle to understand the rules of the game of life and how it can best be played, but most of us are never sure. We look for meaning, but it is elusive. We seek it in our achievements, children, jobs, or social interactions. Many look for it in God. But the scary conclusion to this welter of uncertainty is that nobody knows any of these things for sure. And no matter how we decide to play it, seeds of doubt always remain.

These are the kinds of generalized fears that drive people to join cults. The cult takes care of its adherents and quells their fears. The cult has all the answers as to how one should live life; its members have only to listen and obey. For the believers, all the guesswork is eliminated. Life becomes simple. The uncertainty is dispelled. Just do as the cult prescribes and everything will be fine— no more fears. (However, there may be a few other problems—like cyanide in the Kool-Aid.)

Leaving these global issues aside, there are other reasons for us to develop generalized feelings of insecurity. For example, from the day we are born, we are learning everything from people who can do everything better than we can. They—usually our parents—are bigger, stronger, and know more than we do. They control us physically and mentally, and, during our formative years, actually hold the power of life and death over us. Comparing our weaknesses to their strengths could certainly make one feel a little insecure. At least I know that I have plenty of insecurities and so do all of my friends—facts that would come as no surprise to Adler.

HOW DO FEARS SURFACE IN COMPETITION?

Overlaid upon and interacting with these generalized fears and insecurities is the specific fear of losing. Obviously, a person who is weak, unstable, and strongly beset with generalized insecurities will be more susceptible to the fear of failure in competition than a person who is not. Whenever there is risk of loss, the drives to achieve and win are accompanied by the fear of failure. Why? Because losing is painful. Even if we were not genetically programmed to be fearful in competitive situations (and there is some evidence that we are) we would soon learn to become fearful because losing is so painful, and, as a general rule, pain leads to fear.

WHERE IS THE FEAR LURKING?

To more clearly conceptualize the character of the competitive fear that I have in mind, let us chew on it a little more thoroughly. First, the expression "fear of failure" is somewhat of a misnomer. The dread is not totally of failure itself, but rather of its most important underpinning—the responsibility for failure. People can, to some extent, accept failing. But they wiggle, squirm, bob, weave and duck to avoid its being their fault. We dread what the loss seems to say about us as much as the loss itself. Our deepest competitive fear is that we somehow lack the internal substance to be a winner We fear that the outcome of the contest will expose some character flaw or some loser's weakness in us. We are afraid that we don't have "it", whatever "it" is—the indefinable essence of the ability to succeed.

This is the answer to the mysterious question of why sports competitors "choke" most frequently when they are ahead and on the brink of victory rather than when they are behind and on the brink of defeat. For example, when tennis players are just about to win a difficult match, they often stiffen up, become conservative, miss routine shots, hope their opponents will double fault, and generally make a hash of their opportunities. Basketball teams frequently do the same thing. They may have attained a lead by playing aggressive, fast-moving basketball, but with the game about ready to fall into their hands, they suddenly start to think, slow down, pass the ball around the perimeter and miss their shots. On the basis of pure logic, one would predict that the opposite should occur. Being ahead should make them feel more confident. Surely failure (losing) cannot appear as threatening when one is ahead in score as it does when one is behind. Choking, it would seem, should occur most often on the brink of defeat. After all, it is here that failure (losing) looms largest. Obviously the majority of competitors are afraid of something else.

This something else is the fear that they will fail not through any lack of physical ability but rather because some vital mental attribute is missing. Competitors who have reached the edge of victory have played the game well

47

enough to win. They have done everything physically necessary to win other than actually "winning" itself. And that is where the uncertainty lies. They are now naked before the altar of victory. They subconsciously feel that there is no excuse for losing other than their own inadequacy as competitors or as "winners." Their insecurities may even cause them to anticipate that their opponents are about to unleash yet unseen abilities, and they needlessly change their games—for the worse. Their sum and substance as competitors is being put to the test, and they dare not fail. They are afraid that the test will find them wanting.

ARE PEOPLE REALLY AFRAID OF WINNING?

People have often talked about the fear of winning and have confused this with the fear of failure. Since so many competitors get nervous and falter on the brink of victory, it looks, to the surface observer, as if they are afraid of winning. This is simply not so, for the reasons described above. People are not afraid of winning. On the contrary, they very much want to win. Winning makes them happy afterward, and people do not fear that which makes them happy. They fear that which makes them unhappy, and losing makes them unhappy.

Explanations of why people are afraid of winning generally involve twisted, hypothetical reasoning. This psychobabble proceeds along the lines that the fearful competitors do not feel worthy of victory nor can they shoulder the responsibilities of victory or some such complex, upside-down theory. There is not an ounce of proof for any of this, and it is far simpler and more straightforward to assume the obvious—that they are afraid of losing.

My own experience in tennis tournaments supports this. For example, I was far more likely to feel fear on the brink of victory in an important tournament than in a minor one. At the same time, I was utterly elated after winning a match at Wimbledon and far less so after a victory at the Santa Monica Open. Like everyone else in the world, I enjoyed winning and even more for large rewards than small. So why in the world would I be afraid to win? I have never been afraid of being ecstatically happy. On the other hand, I never much looked forward to the misery and emotional torment of losing, the prospect of which was enough to generate plenty of fear.

FEAR ALSO RUNS RAMPANT
IN THE BUSINESS ARENA

Although fear of failure is closer to the surface in sports (because winning and losing are more immediate and obvious), it is equally omnipresent in the workplace. In sports, the fear is often palpable and physical—the competitor's hands may actually shake under the pressure of the crucial situation, and coordination may fail—whereas in business, the fear is usually deeper, though more subtle, and, at times, equally destructive to performance.

In the workplace, the fear of being a "loser" is even more profoundly frightening than it is in sport because here success or failure is such a core issue. It is where we spend eight hours a day, five days a week. Unlike sports, where we can claim we just play for fun and winning doesn't matter, earning a living is a necessity. We can't avoid it. We must pay our bills and support our families. And who wouldn't like to have a little more money? There is no credible excuse to avoid competing in this arena.

Most people are particularly afraid to display, in front of their friends and associates, any hint of financial ineptitude. It is why asking people how much money they make is such a social taboo. It is also why so many buy more expensive homes, cars, clothes, jewelry, etc., than they can afford and spend their lives choking on credit card debts and suffering under backbreaking monthly payments. It is why being fired from one's job is far more than simply an economic disaster. It attacks one's center as a competent, winning, successful individual.

And to make matters worse, other people are darn nosey about how well we are doing. When you go on vacation your friends are apt to ask where you are staying. They want to know whether you can afford the Ritz Carleton or whether you need a half-priced deal at the Travelodge. They take note of the car you drive, the clothes and accessories you wear, and the home you live in. We are not imagining it. Other people have some interest in where we rank—in business, sports, and all the other areas of achievement—and the possibility that this ranking might be low, that we might be seen as "losers," is frightening.

In business fear can occasionally reach rather high levels. When I started out in the investment business I had a stockbroker acquaintance named Paul Cohen who told me that the thing that got him out of bed in the morning was

49

STARK FEAR. Unpredictable as the brokerage business was, Paul fought against frightening fantasies of quiet telephones, disappearing orders, mounting bills, and unmet mortgage payments. In Paul's case the fear was actually motivating, luckily for him, and simply supplied extra drive for success. He was too frightened to sit around waiting for business to come to him and ended up doing well by hustling to get it. In the many cases of those less fortunate than Paul, however, the fear is drive-sapping and debilitating. Clearly, any serious threat to our financial security—our ability to pay our bills and support our families and ourselves—can be terribly frightening.

PEOPLE TRY TO AVOID THE TEST

Most people do not want to be tested on their abilities to succeed and win. Fear of failure makes the situation too stressful, and high stress is unpleasant. This fact was highlighted recently when I attended the PTR (Professional Tennis Registry) National Convention at Hilton Head, South Carolina, and sat in on a training session for their world-class junior tennis program. It was in the afternoon and thirty to forty prospective young tennis champions were congregated at the courts waiting for the formal program to start. While they waited, a group of them engaged in a heated game of mini-tennis. (This is played by four players in the front half of the court, all shots must bounce before the service line, and no ball may be hit hard.) They were having a wonderful time—dinking the ball at odd angles, running around, laughing, and joking. I was struck by the difference between this and their normal tennis practice session. This was fun and the other is serious work. Here they had nothing to lose or gain, there was no fear of failure, and they could simply run around and have a good time.

WHEN LOSING HURTS THE MOST

This leads to an axiom regarding pain of loss. The harder you try to win, and the more you invest emotionally, the greater the pain of loss.

Winning and losing tennis matches strikes an immediate and resonant emotional chord because it is an individual sport, and the loser walks off the court with his status directly and painfully diminished relative to the victor. Here the emotional responses of the loser are amplified because the underlying nature of a tennis match is a symbolic fight for superiority, and there is a genetic contribution to the fear of failure and the potential pain of loss. For this reason, it is painful and unpleasant to lose almost any tennis match in which one invests a reasonable amount of effort, even if it is just a Sunday afternoon recreational match played solely (supposedly) for exercise and fun.

When I lost a tournament match, I was in agony, sometimes for days. Immediately after the loss, I didn't want to talk to anyone. I felt like hiding in my room, locking the door, and never coming out. No one taught me to feel this way, but it was my invariable and instinctive reaction. I suffered great pain because my investment in winning was total. I was not a great athlete, but I was a perfectionist and did everything possible to improve my chances of winning. I practiced endless hours, concentrated with ferocious intensity, and never gave up, regardless of the score or situation. And when I went down, I went down hard. I sound silly admitting this, but even losing a practice match was enough to ruin my day.

TENNIS IS A SYMBOLIC FIGHT

The emotional framework of a tennis match is the same as that of a fistfight. The only difference is that you are not allowed to actually hit each other. It is a symbolic fight where the antagonists emotionally vie for territory, sex, and status. The winner feels like he gets them all, and the loser feels devastated. I can recall the emotions I had before playing in the finals of an important tournament. I was nervous. I had a feeling of dread and uncertainty. I longed to get it over with, and at the same time, I wanted to put off playing. Sometimes, when it looked like rain might postpone the match, I secretly wished it would pour so I wouldn't have to play that day. I wanted to escape the tension, at least temporarily, and do something pleasant, like go to a movie. But the question is, what was I so afraid of? I had everything to win by playing the final. I could win the tournament. If I lost, I would have been no worse off than not playing. And I certainly was not afraid of being embarrassed. I knew full well that on my worst days, I still played better tennis than anyone in the audience ever dreamed of playing. What I dreaded, in my deepest fiber, was simply BEING BEATEN.

The feelings I experienced before an important tennis match were familiar. I remembered them from childhood. They were the same feelings I suffered sitting in my grammar school class after some kid said he was going to fight me after school and beat me up. The uneasiness, dread, and fear were the same. But what was I afraid of? I was not afraid that the other kid was going to break my nose, smash my face, or put me in the hospital. It was not really the fear of getting hurt at all. It was the fear of BEING BEATEN UP, whatever that meant. I was afraid of having the other kid end up on top of me. I was afraid of losing. I was afraid of being, somehow, disgraced and diminished. And that is the same subliminal fear I had before a tennis match.

51

MIGHT THE FEAR ALSO HAVE A GENETIC ORIGIN?

This fear of failure in competition probably has a genetic as well as a learned basis. Lorenz noticed that fear invariably occurred in conflict situations. For example, his animal studies showed that aggression was always accompanied by fear, leading him to ascribe a genetic component to the fear as well as to the aggression. Lorenz described this phenomenon in cichlids, an aggressive, territorial little fish, whose behavior he spent a great deal of time observing in his aquarium. When a neighbor invades a cichlid's territory, the property owner furiously attacks the interloper, ramming and biting him until he drives the invader away. As the invader retreats, he is pursued by the angry property owner until he is chased into his own territory. As the territorial boundary is reached and passed, the original property owner seems to become more fearful and less aggressive. Simultaneously, the original interloper seems to lose his fear and become aggressive as he now switches from invasion mode to the mode of defending his own territory. He turns, attacks, and chases the other fish back into his own territory. In general, the cichlid's aggression is greater than its fear when it is inside its own territory, and its fear is greater than its aggression when it is in the territory of another cichlid. Lorenz termed this phenomenon "oscillation." The two fish pursue each other back and forth until a steady state is reached on the border of the two territories where aggression and fear in the two fish are balanced.

In fact, it is the balance between fear and aggression that defines the territorial boundary in the first place. Of course, the fish do not perform territorial surveys, and there are no lines drawn along the bottom of the aquarium demarcating a border crossing. It is simply that the fish with the most powerful drive of aggression and the least fear stakes out the largest territory. Territorial size does not relate to the size of the fish. It relates to the aggression-fear balance of the fish. It seems to be the area that the fish perceives as rightfully his and for which, therefore, he is ready to fight. (This sounds a little anthropomorphic. Who knows what the fish really perceives, but this is the way it appears to a human observer.) In a sense, the territorial boundary is an imaginary line created in the mind of the fish that limits its capacity to acquire more property, and the same phenomenon seems to occur in humans.

FEARS REDUCE OUR ACHIEVEMENT LIMITS

A similar phenomenon occurs in tennis matches and is the reason why lesser players have such great difficulty defeating players who are presumed to be better than they are. For example, when Fred, a lower-ranked player at the local tennis club, happens to win the first set from Nick, the club champion, he often lets up in the second set, and Nick ends up winning the match. Why does this happen so often? It happens because Fred perceives Nick to be better than he is. When Fred wins the first set, he feels that he is playing above himself—in a sense, he is out of his own "territory." Like the cichlid, fear now grows and aggression (or in this case, ambition) diminishes. Winning the match for Fred is like entering deeply into foreign "territory." It does not feel like it is rightfully his, so his drive level slips—he eases up.

Nick, on the other hand, sees himself as the better player. To him, winning the match feels like his proper due. When Fred wins the first set, Nick reacts like the cichlid does when a neighbor invades his territory. Nick's aggression (ambition) rises and his fear diminishes. His back is up. He feels that this should not be happening. As Nick's drive increases, he comes roaring back over his weakened opponent and wins the second set. In the third set, with the match at stake, they are playing in Nick's territory, and he has the advantage in the aggression–fear balance. Nick will drive through to finish and win because he thinks he should, and Fred will weaken and lose because he also thinks he should. The outcome is dominated by the self-imposed limits of the two contestants. As the underling in such a contest, it is important to recognize that these personal limits are arbitrary and not real.

ACHIEVEMENT LIMITS OCCUR IN BUSINESS ALSO

Business is another area where the aggression vs. fear balance imposes arbitrary limits. Bert Borman, co-founder of the Pennsylvania Life Insurance Co., monitored the successes and failures of thousands of his employees over twenty-five years, and described to me how the phenomenon worked with his salespeople. Selling insurance is a tough business, but theoretically a good salesperson can make almost unlimited amounts of money. Yet Borman found that few, if any, ever approached what he believed to be their true potential. The same scenario, he claims, played itself out over and over. A carefully recruited salesperson would work diligently to accumulate a book of business. He would start to make a comfortable living but then, for one reason or another, his income would prematurely level off. Sometimes it would be due to personal health, or perhaps the health of a family member; sometimes it involved outside interests; sometimes it was personal or family problems; sometimes it was an affair. Whatever the reason, the result was always the same—the salesperson's income would just stop growing. On a case-by-case basis, Borman found each explanation for this leveling had surface plausabiliy, but over the years, he noticed a clear pattern emerging. "The salespeople seemed to have a preconceived idea of how far they could go," he told me. "Deep down they had a certain income level they felt they should reach. But they didn't dare go any farther, even though almost all of them were quite capable of doing so."

He said that this apparent "topping out" occurred at arbitrary levels of sales that bore little relation to the individual's talent or ability. It was a self-imposed boundary where drive evaporated. Because they did not feel that a higher level of sales was their "due," they became fearful that they would fail. They unconsciously feared that further efforts would prove futile, so they stopped trying. It was as if they were comfortable in their own "territory" of sales and weakened when they contemplated going beyond it. Like the "oscillation" phenomenon in cichlids, the sales person's achievement boundaries are self-imposed and relate to his personal balance between fear and ambition.

WE SABOTAGE OURSELVES

In order to see this more clearly, let's compare two men who earn different salaries. Picture Michael who makes $65,000 per year as the owner of a small business. He has a wife and a couple of kids and lives in a modest three-bedroom home in a middle-level suburb. He has the usual worries about money, but he gets by and is able to afford his present lifestyle. He would like to make more money, but his earnings have stabilized, and he doesn't expend a great deal of energy pushing for a dramatic increase.

Larry has approximately the same educational background and intellectual capability as Michael, but Larry sells commercial real estate and makes an income of $120,000 per year. His home is a spacious four-bedroom model in an affluent suburb, and he is able to afford some of the nicer things in life, like the occasional expensive vacation and sending his two kids to private school. Like Michael, Larry is always pressed for money and would dearly love to make more, but his earnings also seem to have stabilized, and he has, more or less, made peace with his position.

Since both men are constantly pressed for money and want to earn more, one might question why they don't make major efforts to do so. Why do they just accept the situation as it stands? The answer is that Michael and Larry have secured stable economic territories (as identified by their income levels). Within these territories Michael and Larry experience relatively little fear and uncertainty because they know how to make their present incomes. In contrast, making substantially more is a chancy and insecure proposition. They are not sure of how to do it. In order to earn dramatically more money, they would have to leave their economic territories (their comfort zones), and then they would have to directly face their fears of failure. This fear stops them from making major efforts. In a sense, their incomes are functionally capped by their fears. Fears make them accept their present levels of income because to do otherwise would expose them to potential failure, and people avoid fears of failure whenever they can.

Michael and Larry are not simply lacking energy. Both would react powerfully if their normal income levels were threatened. Picture, for example, how Larry would behave if his $120,000 income were cut to $65,000. Now his lifestyle would be threatened. At $65,000 per year Larry would be forced to live at the same economic level as Michael. The difference between them is that Michael accepts this level while Larry, who is accustomed to better, would not. Larry would scramble to reach his former level. He would be powerfully driven to earn more money and would have plenty of energy. Since he has earned $120,000 before, he would not be hindered by fears that earning such an amount is beyond his capabilities. He would be operating within his economic territory, not beyond it. The same thing would happen to Michael if his income were cut to $35,000. Both would be energized and driven to reach their old levels, but once these levels were reached, their energy would dissipate and fear would again predominate (like the cichlids when they reach their territorial boundaries).

Of course fear is not the only reason that people so often lose their drive in either in business or sports after reaching comfortably high levels of performance. If the process of reaching a higher level involves unpleasantness, people may opt out simply because they are not willing to endure the difficulties when they don't feel they have to. Even here, however, fear of failure usually plays some role in limiting performance, and in most cases, it plays the decisive one.

FEAR IS ALSO LEARNED

Although Lorenz believed that fear in conflict situations was genetic, it is clear that some of it must be learned as well. This is because pain causes fear, and anyone who has competed hard and lost knows that losing is painful. It does not take long to learn that competing for anything worthwhile is an uncertain proposition. If the prize is valuable, there will be plenty of others trying hard to get it too. And try as we may, we often find out that they are simply better than we are. We lose. Ouch! Soon we have developed a fear of failure in this competitive situation which ultimately generalizes to other competitive situations. In animal studies, learned fear in response to pain occurs quickly. Give a rat an electric shock when he steps on a metal grid, and he immediately learns to avoid stepping on the grid. Similarly, most people learn to avoid competing with 100 percent intensity quite quickly after suffering a few painful losses.

FEAR OF FAILURE CAN SOMETIMES HELP US ACHIEVE

The reader might ask the obvious question: If fear of failure is such an all-pervasive and generally destructive human condition, why are some people, fearful as they may be, able to achieve so much? For example, John MacEnroe described in his autobiography how he always feared that he was going to lose, even when he had garnered substantial leads over opponents. He never felt that he could relax. His fear drove him to concentrate and work harder to finish an opponent off rather than to ease up when he was ahead. Sallie Krawcheck, the 37 old stock analyst who was recently hired as CEO of Smith Barney and who is one of the most powerful rising stars of the corporate world, admits that she is "incredibly insecure" and fearful that she will not be successful in winning the approbation of her colleagues. Yet, she handles herself with apparent ease and confidence and can point to an almost unbroken string of business successes. These and other successful people are certainly not free from fear of failure.

In the next chapter, we will look more deeply into how fear effects our abilities to compete and achieve.

THE UNCONSCIOUS STRUGGLE BETWEEN AMBITION AND FEAR

Unconcious fear of failure distorts the will to win by altering perceptions and causing competitors to lie to themselves, make excuses, blame others, procrastinate, fail to finish tasks, and panic on the verge of victory.

The scene is the lush grass of the stadium court at Forest Hills in 1961. It is the round of 16 in the US National Championships (now called the US Open). I am drenched with sweat on this muggy, hot, New York afternoon, as I scramble after Whitney Reed's weird assortment of shots. Shadows are beginning to encroach on the court, making the ball more difficult to pick up. But I don't care. I am upset. I concentrate in fits and starts, playing some games well and just smacking balls around in others. Anger wells up, souring my stomach, and I whack the ball as hard as I can. The anger recedes, and I play some good points. I am frustrated and feel like punching somebody, but, of course, that is out of the question. I am not that crazy. But I am crazy enough to stay angry all through the match, even though I know that it will cause me to lose.

Why am I doing this? It is a big situation and a wonderful opportunity for me. In the previous round Whitney had upset Chuck McKinley, who was really the best American in the tournament and the guy I did not want to play. Whitney, on the other hand, was good, but not great, and eminently beatable, particularly since I was coming off a very successful summer tour. I had won the National Intercollegiate singles, the Tri-State Championship (a major tournament on the midwest clay circuit) at Cincinnati, and the Meadow Club Championship (a major tournament on the eastern grass circuit leading up to Forest Hills) at Southampton. I had beaten some of the top players in the world and had been named to the U.S. Davis Cup team. Now I have a great chance to make the quarterfinals of the National Championships and possibly even the semis or finals. I have every reason to want to win, yet I can't seem to shake my anger and get my emotions under control. What could make me angry enough to act so contrary to my own best interests?

The night before the match, my wife and I had gotten into an argument (the subject of which I dare not relate because it was embarrassingly petty), and I walked onto the stadium court the next day still stewing about it. When the match started, I was immediately testy. Everything irritated me, and I had difficulty staying focused and calm. All I could think about was how angry I was at my wife. I brooded, "How could she have had so little consideration as to upset me like this just before such an important match?" "She ruined my concentration," I fumed. I lost in four sets and came off the court convinced that my wife had subverted my golden opportunity to win the tournament.

It was not until years later that I understood the truth. I had lost the match because I had fallen victim to the most basic problem of competition, the factor that thwarts most people in their quest for success—the unconscious conflict between the desire for success and the fear of failure. To escape this conflict, we construct various defense mechanisms that reduce our anxieties by clouding our minds. Unfortunately, though they may make us feel better, these defense mechanisms also make us poor competitors. At this point, we will take a closer look at the workings of these defense mechanisms, and then we will revisit that unfortunate afternoon at Forest Hills with new insight.

WHAT ARE DEFENSE MECHANISMS?

First identified by Sigmond Freud, defense mechanisms are unconscious distortions of perception and interpretation that act to protect us from unpalatable facts and fears. Cold reality can sometimes be too unpleasant to bear. Reality may force us to face our own inadequacies and fears, deal with desires and actions that may conflict with our moral upbringings or self-images, or accept stressful conflicts that we cannot resolve. At these times, it is comforting to change things around in our minds so that these conflicts can appear to go away.

WE FORGET ON PURPOSE

Repression is one type of defense mechanism identified by Freud. Here one selectively and conveniently "forgets" facts that are difficult to deal with consciously. Freud naturally used sexual examples. These generally involved patients who had sexual experiences that were too awful to think about, so they were thrust into their unconscious minds and forgotten, that is, until Freud drew them out under hypnosis or through deep talking therapy. I think Freud went too far by seeing sexuality behind every tree and bush, but the general concept of repression certainly has merit.

I can personally recall putting off telephone calls that I did not, for some reason, want to make and then forgetting all about them. Maybe they were important, but they were unpleasant, so I unconsciously pushed them into the recesses of my mind, and they disappeared. By contrast, if someone were going to give me a million dollars if I made a phone call, you can rest assured that I would never forget to make the call. By the same token, my son often forgets to clean his room but rarely forgets to collect his allowance.

MAKING THE PICTURE LOOK BETTER

Freud's other applicable defense mechanism is called "rationalization." Again it works unconsciously but involves conveniently rearranging facts rather than forgetting them. And, again, it is a form of self-delusion. Here, as with all defense mechanisms, an original set of facts may be unpleasant to face. This time we create a more attractive overall picture by restructuring the facts and changing our viewpoints. In the process, we may reduce the importance of some facts while amplifying the importance of others (all unconsciously, of course). We don't simply make up false facts; we just change the emphasis of real ones. Facts that are inconvenient to the picture we want to see may be forgotten, while more convenient ones are brought to center stage. The final picture is designed to make us feel better and/or to reduce conflicts that would remain unresolved if the original (true) picture were kept intact.

An early example of this phenomenon in literature appears in Aesop's fable of the fox and the grapes. The essence of the story is that the fox, finding that he is unable to reach a bunch of grapes, concludes that they are "sour" anyway. Since "sour" grapes are no great loss, the fox feels better about not getting them and thus reconciles the discrepancy between his desires and his abilities. As with all defense mechanisms, the crucial factor is that the fox completely believes the story he has made up, a belief made possible because there are usually elements of truth in it. His unconscious mind has restructured the situation without his being consciously aware of it, and, as most of us will do if we are not very careful, the fox believes his own bull...t.

WE CAN SEE THEM WORKING

Psychologists usually suspect that defense mechanisms are operating when a person's actions appear counter-productive—that is, when they carry a person in a direction directly opposed to his or her stated goals. There is a reason for everything. People do not act randomly. We may not know what is motivating a certain behavior, but something is certainly causing it to take one direction over another. The reasons may not be good or productive ones, but they are reasons nevertheless. When this happens, people are usually satisfying some unconscious need that they are unwilling to face and consciously accept.

DEFENSE MECHANISMS DUPED
ME AT FOREST HILLS

Now, a little too late, unfortunately, the reason why I was so irrationally angry that day in the stadium is clear. The whole affair had been an example of defense mechanisms in action—rationalization, in particular. I had played too many tournaments in a row that summer, and the continuous stress had weakened me mentally. I was tired of competing and looking for a way out. I did not have the stomach to face the prolonged pressure of a crucial three-out-of-five set match on the stadium court. I had had enough and was subconsciously seeking an excuse to escape. The argument with my wife was real, albeit silly, but my unconscious mind purposefully exaggerated my reaction to it. And it was because of this exaggeration that I could cast away responsibility for winning the match. My psychological gain was to relieve myself of responsibility and stress, but the cost was to throw away my chances to win a major championship. In hindsight, this was a bad bargain, as it usually is when defense mechanisms poke their ugly noses into competition.

THEY LIE HIDDEN EVERYWHERE

Defense mechanisms are insidious and come in a thousand disguises. When they appear in sports or other areas of competition, they are almost invariably driven by fear. Their hidden purpose is to reduce stress, relieve the individual of responsibility, and lessen the pain of loss. In tennis, for example, satisfying these psychological needs causes players to lose lots of matches. Figuratively speaking, most people compete with one foot on the accelerator and the other on the brake. They want to win but know, at some level, that losing will make them unhappy. As noted earlier, the harder you try and the more deeply you commit yourself to winning, the more painful it will be if you lose. People fear this pain, and to avoid it, many compete with less than a wholehearted commitment. Instead, they rationalize.

Sue at the club tells herself that she doesn't care whether she wins or not—that she is just playing for the exercise, the social interactions, the love of the game, the feeling of hitting the occasional great shot, or just a good suntan. She tells herself that winning doesn't matter. Of course she is lying to herself. Everyone would prefer winning to losing. It may not be practical to pay the emotional or physical price required to win every match, but that doesn't mean winning would not be more fun than losing. Sue doesn't want to accept this. Doing so would put her under pressure during the match (which is not much fun, I must admit) and put her at risk of feeling badly if she loses. The price Sue pays for avoiding this unpleasantness is to become a less effective competitor and lose frequently. At the same time, Sue has the niggling feeling that she really would like to win and that she is kidding herself. As a consequence, she inhabits a competitive "grey" world where she doesn't try too hard to win, but doesn't feel too bad when she loses (which is often), and doesn't feel too proud of herself either.

A better alternative would be for Sue to admit to herself that she wants to win but that there are simply some occasions when she is not up to competing with 100 percent intensity. It may be too much work, and she may not be prepared for the pressure and unpleasantness. At such times she will simply not do so. (After all, nobody is holding a gun to her head.) On the other hand, she doesn't have to lie to herself about her motives either. Facing the truth gives Sue control of the situation. Otherwise, she will forever be passively responding to forces of whose existence she is unaware. And on those other occasions when she has the stomach for it, she can decide she wants to win and test herself by doing everything in her power (within the rules) to do so. Here she risks feeling badly if she loses, but what the heck, she'll get over it. And she will greatly improve her results. (Test question: Who has the best chance of winning a long, tough match played on a hot day—the player who says she is playing for the pleasant feeling of hitting the ball hard, or the player who overtly acknowledges that she wants to win the match?)

DEFENSE MECHANISMS AT SCHOOL

As a student at UCLA, I joined a fraternity. I was not much of a "joiner" kind of guy, but the fraternity house provided me with a place to live on campus, even though I spent most of my time at class, on the tennis court, or in the library. During my forays into the frat house, I frequently noticed "Jerry" (fictitious name) hanging around, playing ping-pong, philosophizing about life with his fraternity brothers, drinking beer, listening to music, or whatever. Jerry was good-looking, an excellent athlete, and an extremely bright guy, yet unaccountably insecure. He hid his fears behind a facade of "coolness." I recall him proudly proclaiming to me on several occasions that he had "not cracked a book or been to class all semester."

The next semester I was not terribly surprised to learn that Jerry had failed out of school. He may have consoled himself with the fact that he hadn't tried, so his failure was not a smear on his intelligence, but a university degree would have better served his interests.

NOT EVEN TENNIS CHAMPIONS ARE IMMUNE

Tennis champions also succumb to defense mechanisms occasionally, although no true champion does so too often. (The average person, by contrast, succumbs all the time.) Goran Ivanisevic tanked to Pete Sampras in the finals at Wimbledon in 1994, throwing the third set 6-0 after losing the first two sets in tie-breakers. What was Ivanisevec's gain in deciding to do this? Since there could have been no rational, conscious, or productive motive, it must have satisfied some unconscious need of which Ivanisevic himself was unaware. He got something out of it (we will shortly discuss exactly what that was), and that something was pretty powerful since it was, to him, worth throwing away his chances to win an extra $400,000, a world championship, and a coveted place in the history books of tennis.

And while he was throwing the match away, his mind was busy rationalizing. He was reconstructing the facts so that at that moment, tanking seemed, to him, like the most reasonable thing in the world to do. At the same time, in some corner of his brain, he probably had a vague sense that tanking was crazy, but this rationality was not powerful enough to overcome his destructive, self-delusional impulses. (Fortunately, for Ivanisevic, he seemed to have finally learned from this experience. He won the 2001 Wimbledon championship by never wavering or giving up in his matches, despite bad calls and choking and double faulting in a number of crucial situations.)

HOW ABOUT COLLEGE TENNIS PLAYERS?

Other examples appear at every level of tennis. Eddie Edwards, a member of my Pepperdine tennis team in the late 1970s and ultimately a professional ranked among the top 100 players in the world, often experienced a variation on the problem we discussed in Chapter Four—that of finishing off opponents when he was ahead. His pattern was to win the first set, develop a lead in the second set, and then ease off. This would allow his opponent to catch up, and

Eddie would eventually find himself in a death-struggle for the third set, which too often went against him.

Eddie came off the court after losing one of these matches telling me, "Coach, I just can't seem to concentrate when I get ahead. I get up, and I feel so over-confident that I hardly try. I relax, and the next thing I know I'm in the third set." My response was that Eddie could not really have been over-confident, even though he claimed he was, because he had been in this situation many times in the past and had lost plenty of matches by relaxing. He certainly knew from bitter experience that he was capable of losing the match. What distortion of reality, then, led Eddie to believe that he was overconfident?

Eddie's problem was one of the most common in sports—lowering one's standard of play when one is on the brink of victory. As so often happens with athletes in this situation, Eddie's fears of failure threatened to surface as the issue of actually winning the match occupied more and more of his view-screen. Eddie was under-confident, not over-confident. Knowing, at some level, that his opponent was dangerous and could turn the match around in an instant filled the situation with pressure, and this pressure grew as the end of the match neared. Subconsciously, Eddie wanted to escape this mounting pressure. As we discussed in the previous chapter, the "moment of truth" is when one is ahead and passes or fails the test of actually winning the match. It is here that the test looms psychologically large and the pressure and stress levels rise.

Eddie's method of reducing stress was to subconsciously procrastinate doing the dirty job of finishing. Instead of girding himself mentally for the increasingly stressful push to the finish, Eddie went on cruise control—his way of checking out. Unbeknownst to himself, Eddie was relying on the match falling into his lap so that he could be spared the risky unpleasantness of doing the work himself. The "relaxation" and "overconfidence" he felt were really Eddie's way of rationalizing. He was lying to himself. Eddie was really trying to avoid, albeit temporarily, a situation which was about to become increasingly nasty. Like the conservative gambler who gets ahead, Eddie (subconsciously) wanted to pocket his winnings and get away from the table before his luck turned. He was fearful of taking further risks and failing at this most crucial juncture.

TENNIS PLAYERS AREN'T THE ONLY SELF-DELUDERS

Drive-sapping rationalizations are a danger in any sport at any level and may, in fact, have cost skater Debbie Thomas her chance for a gold medal at the

Calgary Olympic Games. Her rival for the gold, Katarina Witt, was known to be a warrior on the ice. Everyone was aware of her ferocious drive to compete and win. Witt was already an Olympic champion when, two years before the Calgary Olympics, Debbie Thomas upset her at the World Championship. After that Witt's attitude was, "You took what was mine, and I'm going to take it back." The next year at the World Championships, held in Thomas' home-town of Cincinnati, Thomas put on a great performance, but Witt put on an even better one and won. Witt's aggressive desire to win seemed to deflate and intimidate Thomas. As the Olympics impended the following year, Thomas began to think defensively and rationalize with talk about going to medical school. Witt, meanwhile, talked about winning the gold, and by the time the Olympics began, the outcome was never in doubt.

BUSINESS PEOPLE ALSO SUCCUMB

Of course, competitive athletics is not the only venue where defense mechanisms reduce our effectiveness. Unconscious fear of failure and its attendant defenses are ever-present dangers in business as well. In business the outcomes are generally less clear-cut than they are in sports, and the situations have more variables, so it is easier to obscure the workings of defense mechanisms. Nonetheless, fear of failure is still a hidden danger at all levels of business.

Consider the situation where people are faced with new projects, and, because the projects are new, there is some degree of uncertainty associated with their outcomes. Without a firm deadline (and, often, even with one), most people are likely to procrastinate completing the projects, even though the degree of uncertainty might be minimal and the people perfectly capable of figuring out what to do. The projects will tend to end up on the back burners. This is because the uncertainty of outcome generates enough hidden fear to make people procrastinate completion as long as possible. If, on the other hand, these people had completed similar projects in the past and were comfortable with exactly how they should be done, they would not now hesitate.

I noted a specific example of this in a small business that I used to own. We produced specialty food products, among which was a line of low-fat salad dressings that we sold to supermarkets. I became aware that we were getting some returns on one of our dressings because there was occasional minor leak-age when some of our containers were stored tilted instead of upright. Although the problem was not severe, it was clear that it ultimately needed fix-ing. So I instructed Martha, our head of wholesale operations, to look into the situation and get an alternative container. Time passed and the project didn't get done. I occasionally questioned Martha on its progress, and she said she was waiting for price quotes or samples from suppliers or other information, meanwhile she was busy with the rest of her job. Finally, I realized that at its present rate of progress the project was not going to be finished before the next ice age.

To speed the process I sat down with Martha, and, together, we laid out all the steps necessary to get the new containers in our hands. We wrote out a summary chart listing all suitable container types, their costs, shipping times, minimum order quantities, etc., and made a decision on which one to buy. We wrote out a similar chart for the lids and decided on a lid as well. The only thing left was to write out an action plan for redesigning and printing our labels, and we did this also. All instructions were specific, and my concurrence made decisions less stressful. The pressure was off Martha. Within days orders were placed, and within a month we had our new containers.

Martha was experienced and highly intelligent and could have easily completed this project without my help. Why didn't she? Instead, months of data gathering and dawdling went by. Martha certainly made some efforts on the project, but not the concerted one necessary for an expedient finish. She confused herself by mixing this project with her other tasks. She worked on it in fits and starts, proceeding with pieces of the project and then doing something else. The relative importance of each task was not assessed, and Martha was not aware that she was deliberately putting off finishing the container project. She did this because there were decisions to be made, and she was on uncharted ground. She could not see all the way to the end of the project and was vaguely uncertain of its outcome. Doubt subconsciously tempted her to take up familiar and comfortable tasks first.

This syndrome is common in people who do not finish projects that are assigned to them by their bosses. (It is even common with projects that company owners don't finish, although company owners usually overcome uncertainties and expeditiously finish projects, otherwise they would not, for long, be company owners.) The bosses often have difficulty understanding why some employees do not follow instructions and finish assigned tasks. The employees frequently do not finish because of hidden fear. They are simply unsure of exactly how to do the tasks. This uncertainty makes them fearful, and the fear makes them procrastinate. Bosses can overcome this, at times, by providing more detailed instructions, including exact specifications of each step needed to complete the project.

Another method that often helps circumvent the unconscious fear factor associated with a new project is to assign two or more people to it. (Notice that I say "new" project because people are not usually fearful of projects they have completed in the past.) Since human beings are a communal species, there is comfort in numbers. We are more likely to fear the unknown when we are alone than with a group. Moreover, in a group, blame for failure can be shared. (In tennis, for example, doubles is far less nerve-wracking than singles because there is a partner available with whom to share the responsibility for a potential loss.) In summary, "group comfort" can reduce the inertia caused by the fear of failure and can make it easier for a group to get started on and complete a complex project than for an individual.

I HAD TO DEAL WITH MY PLAYERS' FEARS

When I began coaching at Pepperdine, I thought the job just entailed passing on my years of accumulated tennis knowledge to an eager young team. I had developed techniques, drills, and strategies that were very effective in turning me into a world-class player. I felt they would be equally effective with my team. To my surprise, I found that the job of coaching was 10 percent teaching tennis and 90 percent dealing with irrationality and defense mechanisms. I saw the unconscious fear of failure behind most problems, and it became my job to cut through self-delusional excuses, a common variety of defense mechanism, and force my players to compete without them.

I was effective at wringing maximum performance out of my young charges by simply not accepting excuses. When they tried them on me, they learned to expect responses from me like, "So what?" "That's not going to help you," and "Forget it and get back to business." Sympathy, benevolent as it may appear when a problem is real, is often counterproductive. It promotes self-pity and weakens people. It is like throwing someone a liferaft when he (or she) is sinking in a sea of fears and allowing him to cling to it when his only true salvation is to swim with all his strength for the nearest shore. Sympathy can be like candy. People want it, but it is not good for them.

A typical situation occurred when one of my players thought he got a bad line call from an opponent or a linesman. I might have been on the sideline, seen where the ball landed, and also felt that the call was, in fact, a bad one. In most cases I would not tell my player he was gypped out of the point, even though he was. I usually said something like, "Play on," "Get over it," or "Win the next point." To acknowledge the bad call and to sympathize would have tempted my player to dwell on it, divert his attention from the task at hand, and lose additional points. We cannot expect the world to be fair and the playing field to be level. It isn't and never will be. Devoting our efforts to leveling the playing field or decrying the fact that it is not level dissipates our drive and causes us to lose. All we do is confuse the issue in order to cushion the blow of the loss.

EARNING A LIVING IS SCARY

Excuses and defense mechanisms cause us difficulty in all areas of achievement and competition, not the least of which is our ability to obtain and excel in our jobs. As we discussed in the last chapter, failure here is particularly debilitating. People who cannot earn reasonable livings and take care of their families feel disgraced. Like Paul Cohen, when we start out in business, most of us are afraid that we are not going to make it. (And this uncertainty usually remains until and unless we are able to reach the higher levels of business and acquire some financial security.) In the meantime, we must shove our fears aside and drive ourselves to hustle and work hard. We have to. Our bills must be paid. With no alternatives, fear or no fear, we have to figure out how to make a living—how to provide economic value to the capitalistic society in which we live. Having one's back to the wall has a remarkable way of sharpening the senses and clearing the mind. But, if we were offered an escape hatch, the strongest of us would be likely to take it.

Self-deluding excuses occur in the business world as frequently as they do on the tennis courts, often appearing as claims of "unfairness" on the part of superiors or powers that be. People may feel that they have been passed over for promotions or raises simply because superiors do not like them or don't properly appreciate their excellent contributions or skills. This sort of thinking may even be true—so what? It is poisonous because it provides its adherents with excuses that sap their drive.

Of course the world is full of unfairness, and it always will be. Any particular incident may or may not be an example of it, but focusing and dwelling on a presumption of unfairness is counterproductive. It takes your eye off the ball. Such concerns do not help you. If you think the boss is holding you back for personal reasons, react by getting better at your job. Improve. Become more valuable. This will help the boss like you more.

The playing field will never be completely level. If we insist on waiting for a level playing field before we put our disadvantages mentally behind us and get down to wholehearted competition, we are going to be waiting for a long time!

67

Tennis players get bad calls. That is unfair. But unfairly losing occasional points is part of the game. Which strategy is more productive: (1) Expend one's energies in hopelessly trying to get the umpire to change his decision, while bitching for the rest of the afternoon about how one has been cheated, or (2) immediately put the bad call out of mind and focus all of one's energies on winning the rest of the points and on winning the match itself? It's fairly obvious. If one is to compete effectively in tennis, one must accept bad calls as a fact of life and get on with the rest of the match. If a person can't do this, he or she should play another game (like checkers), where one can't get bad calls.

The same strategy holds in business. Our good friends may think they are doing us a favor by listening to our stories of how we have been disadvantaged by factors beyond our control and by agreeing with us. But they are not. Encouraging us to focus on unfair treatment or bad luck simply magnifies these issues out of all proportion to their real economic effects. It does not help the situation. Quite the contrary. It is the wrong message, accurate or inaccurate as it may be, because its psychological effects are debilitating.

All of us are sufficiently insecure to run for shelter, if shelter from fear of competitive failure were offered. (Most working people, at one time or another, weary of the daily struggle to perform, fantasize about escaping the pressures of the rat race. I certainly did when I was in business.) So individuals who feel that they have been wronged have every incentive to exchange risky competitive strife for comfortable positions as victims. They are no longer responsible. They no longer have to overcome the fears, uncertainties, and difficulties of making it in our stressful society. Who wouldn't take this bargain? They can replace the frightening obligation to perform with a dose of self-pity, anger, and resentment. Unfortunately, this does not take into account the fact that self-esteem and happiness, in business as in sports, come from achievement, not from having plausible reasons for why failure was not our fault. Excuses and rationalizations, be they in sport, business, or any other area, provide a comforting path to nowhere.

PART TWO

HOW THE
CHAMPIONS
DO IT

So far we have been exploring, on a philosophical basis, the elements that drive us to compete and achieve, as well as those that hinder our success. Now for the important practical function of this book—that is to help the readers become more successful at competing and achieving. The following 10 chapters will identify the fundamental techniques of champions and will highlight exactly how they function.

I often use the term "champion." I use it to denote those people who are successful at whatever they do. This may be in business, sports, academia, the professions or elsewhere. As examples I frequently use individuals who have made great deals of money or who have become world famous athletes. I do this only because the success of these people is obvious and dramatic. Their stories are inherently interesting. But by my definition, people could be champions if they excelled in any area, no matter how mundane. Teachers, truck drivers, data processors, factory workers, or janitors could be champions if they did their work with exceptional competence.

ANYBODY CAN DO IT

Most of the champion's attitudes and techniques, once they are understood, can be applied by anybody. Anybody can improve and become more successful in business, sports, or elsewhere by becoming aware of their own achievement shortcomings—their counter-productive attitudes and insidiously harmful fears and emotions—and overcoming them by consciously behaving more like the champions. Sure, the champions have it easier because they have better control over their fears and habitually do the right thing competitively, but with enlightenment, discipline, and persistence, the average person can do just as well.

GOAL ORIENTATION

The champions clearly indentify goals and
set up game plans to achieve them.

GOALS YIELD DIRECTION, MOTIVATION, AND GAME PLANS

Champions are more clearly aware of their achievement goals than most people. They fix their goals firmly and distinctly in their view-screens and can thus direct and focus their efforts more effectively. Having a clear goal allows them to develop an intelligent game plan for reaching that goal, and the advancing prospect of reaching it energizes them. Having clear goals and plans allows them to break tasks up into bite-sized pieces and work on them systematically. In this way, it is easier to see to the end of them; they appear less daunting, engender less fear, and are less likely to be put off. Most people, because they are afraid that they will not be able to achieve worthy goals in any case, run blindly and inefficiently with neither clear goals nor developed plans for achievement.

HAVING GOALS AND MOVING TOWARDS THEM MAKES US HAPPY

Not only does setting goals help us become more effective achievers, but it also makes us happier! As noted earlier, people are happiest when they are progressing toward a goal—when they wake up today a little better off than they were yesterday. People who are trapped in situations where improvement is difficult or impossible are less happy. Here the feeling of stagnation is unpleasant and emotionally debilitating. And progressing toward a goal requires, first and foremost, that we have one.

I encountered this phenomenon recently while talking to a young friend who runs a local outlet for a major auto rental company. Jeff (not his real name) told me he was unhappy, yet outward appearances would have suggested that he shouldn't be. Jeff is thirty years old, a former collegiate level athlete, bright, good looking, socially adept, and, after five years, has worked his way up to local outlet manager with an income of $55,000 per year. This doesn't seem too bad, considering that Jeff graduated from a mediocre university with an undistinguished academic record and no marketable skills. He is doing better than most people. Moreover, he is single, has a beautiful girl friend, spends pleasant weekends at the beach and on the tennis courts, and is living quite comfortably. What's the rub?

The problem is that Jeff feels that his income and position with the company have topped out. He sees no future in staying where he is but doesn't know what to do as an alternative. His insecurities and fears of the unknown keep him in place. Though miserable, at least he is safe. He would like to be more entrepreneurial, but lacking both capital and experience, Jeff can see no clear way to go about it. He hesitates simply jumping into another business because he would have to start at the bottom, absorb a tremendous cut in income, and would still have no guarantee of when, if ever, he would make significant money.

Meanwhile, Jeff entertained and quickly discarded thoughts of returning to school for an MBA. His college grades were mediocre, so getting admitted and making his way through a rigorous academic program would be problematic, even if he had the extra money (which he doesn't) to pay his way for the years it would take him to earn the degree. Anyway, he didn't like school in the first place and would not, at this stage, be enamored with several more years of it. All this mental rumination has paralyzed Jeff, trapped between his stagnant job at the car agency and his fears of the unknown.

Jeff is unhappy because day after day passes and his situation remains the same. Without realistic, tangible goals or plans, he feels immobilized. Oh sure, he knows he wants to make more money, but he can't figure out how to do it. As he sees it, he is simply getting older, but no better.

Jeff and I discussed the matter, and I suggested that he re-examine the idea of returning to school for an MBA. Having acknowledged his fears of simply jumping into the unknown, Jeff needed a positive goal that would give him some modicum of security. An MBA was just such a goal. Moreover,

Pepperdine University offers a night program aimed at people just like him, who work days, want to keep their jobs, and cannot attend school full-time. His successful work experience will help him get in. Additionally, he is a different person now than he was ten years ago, when, as an immature kid, he thought universities were simply good places to get tennis scholarships, attend beer busts, chase pretty coeds, and crib on exams. Now, after ten years of living in the real world—working for a paycheck, managing an office and controlling six other people, and meeting personal obligations—he has a new perspective. In my opinion, the new Jeff will do fine academically. This time around he will appreciate the utility of the information and may even (perish the thought) enjoy some of his classes. Finally, the average salary of new Pepperdine MBAs is about $75,000, so Jeff won't have to start at the bottom with a new company and starve.

After thinking it over, Jeff has decided to pursue his MBA, and he already feels better. He learned that his company will help him with tuition costs, and, once he completes the MBA program, it will offer him a substantial increase in salary and more opportunity for promotion. He is optimistic as he makes his detailed plans because he can visualize his life becoming better as he works toward a viable goal. Jeff was never held in place by fear of hard work; rather, it was fear of the unknown. He is happy to work, as long as it is towards a goal he thinks he can reach.

ATTAINING GOALS REDUCES THE FEAR OF FAILURE

Jeff was held in place, partially, by self-doubts. He was unhappy but secure in his position at the car rental company. He was not confident that he could simply jump ship and make a go of it in a new and unknown area. The familiar expressions such as "self-doubt," "lack of confidence," "lack of self-esteem," and "fear of failure" apply here. They are all conceptually similar and represent different ways of describing the same problem—having fears and insecurities that reduce our drive and even paralyze us, that disorient and confuse us, and that prompt us to make emotionally determined, self-protective, and counter-productive decisions. Anything we can do to reduce them will help us become more effective achievers. (In the discussion that follows, I will use these expressions interchangeably in order to make my arguments more readily comprehensible.)

Let's start by looking at confidence. What is confidence, and what makes a person confident? Confidence is merely an expectation of success. And what generally creates expectations of any kind?—past history. For example, we are

73

extremely confident that the sun will come up tomorrow. Why?—because in our lifetimes, and for the preceding several billion years, it always has come up. But what would our expectations be if the sun came up only occasionally—maybe one morning out of ten? Of course we would not be at all confident that it is going to come up tomorrow. Consider our confidence in competitive sports. If we have, in the past, lost many more tennis matches than we have won, how confident will we be that we are going to win our next tennis match? Not very. On the other hand, if we happened to have recently won Wimbledon and have a huge backlog of victories behind us, we would, of course, feel quite differently. Likewise, if we have run a successful business in the past, we suspect that our next business venture will also be successful—and so on.

The simple conclusion is that success breeds confidence. Achieving goals in the past increases our confidence that we will achieve goals in the future. But does success in one area make us confident of success in another? Chapter One suggests that there is likely some confidence carryover, but it is also obvious that the carryover will be greatest where the areas are the most similar. Championship tennis players will have the most confidence carryover in other racquet sports (like racquetball or badminton), less carryover in basketball, and still less in running a business. Yet the ability to succeed itself does seem to generalize, so successful achievement in any area will, to some extent, increase one's overall level of self-confidence.

Pursuing this theme, I would propose that a history of successfully achieving goals will reduce one's fear of failure, decrease self-doubts, increase one's self-esteem, and make one more confident (since all of these expressions refer to the same core issue). And because fear of failure is so detrimental to one's ability to achieve, anything that reduces it will be greatly beneficial. That is why identifying and achieving goals—any goals—is so valuable. When it comes to building self-esteem, simply having other people tell you that you are great is a poor substitute for actual achievement. True self-esteem (aka: self-confidence, reduced fear of failure, reduced self-doubt, or whatever else you want to call it) comes from real achievement. Notwithstanding all the unproven assertions of the self-esteem psychologists to the contrary, this is a deep, subconscious emotional feeling based on one's history of success and cannot be inserted by talk alone.

RICHARD HATCH SHOWS HOW TO WIN ON THE "SURVIVOR" SHOW

Some time ago, as I watched the concluding episode of the television series, "Survivor One," I was struck by how setting clear goals provides a competitive advantage. After the show, Bryant Gumbel hosted a follow-up show where all the contestants were gathered together, and they discussed their experiences and responded to comments and questions as to how they played the game. The strategies that the winner, Richard Hatch, used contrasted sharply with those of the losing contestants, and this difference struck me as an excellent example of how the winners get the best of the losers with their more effective goal-setting techniques. But for readers not familiar with the show, let's start with a little background.

WHAT WAS THE "SURVIVOR" SHOW ALL ABOUT?

This was the first airing of the "Survivor" show concept, and it took the country by storm, attracting a huge television viewing audience and frenzied media and commercial attention. It was "real" TV, where 16 real people, not actors, were put on a secluded tropical island and directed to play a game in which the winner would collect $1,000,000. The group attended periodic "tribal councils" at which one of them was voted off the island, and the object of the game was to be the last person remaining. The winner was the survivor, and he or she would collect $1,000,000 in cash. That is an imposing prize and certainly sufficient to motivate most of us to try to get our hot hands on it.

The situation was interesting because the contestants were put under stress. They were given insufficient food, had to build their own shelter, and were forced to endure rain, heat, rats, snakes, insects, and a variety of diabolical contests instituted by the producers of the show. And tired, hungry, insect bitten, sleep deprived, and uncomfortable people have difficulty maintaining their mental defenses or hiding their true personalities. They had to live and work together for common goals, while periodically disposing of one of their fellow contestants with their votes, all the while avoiding being voted off themselves. It was a tricky, well-constructed game that ultimately turned selfish, duplicitous, and nasty. Human nature reared its ugly head.

WHY DID RICHARD HATCH WIN?

The winner was Richard Hatch, a 39-year-old corporate consultant, and an excellent example of what this chapter is about. Since this was the first of the series of "Survivor" shows, none of these contestants had the benefit of watching earlier shows to see how the game might best be played. Contestants on "Survivor Two" and later shows could use Hatch's strategies because they knew that they worked. Hatch, on the other hand, had to figure them out himself in a bewilderingly new set of circumstances. Winning this game made him a champion by my definition, but, of course, being a champion does not mean that he was a nice guy or admirable character, just that he is good at winning.

Richard Hatch is a poster-boy for the effectiveness of setting clear goals and adopting a practical and intelligent game plan. Rich (as he was known on the show) behaved differently from almost all of the other contestants in that he clearly identified his goal beforehand—to win the $1,000,000—and he never lost sight of it. His actions were, at all times and under all circumstances, directed toward achieving this goal. This entailed devising an effective game plan before ever arriving on the island and carrying it out persistently and intelligently. His 15 rivals for the money were amateurs. He was a professional.

Rich consciously acknowledged at the outset that he was there to win, not to make friends, sightsee, have an adventure, or get on television. He realized that the weekly vote was the key and, in order to insure that he was on the right side of it, he decided to immediately and secretly ally himself with a small group of trustworthy comrades who would agree to vote as a block. As founder and leader of the "alliance," he was soon able to vote off the island anyone he chose. As additional security, he was determined to make himself useful by augmenting the group's scanty food supply with fish that he caught daily. Thus armed and by playing off one contestant against another, Rich managed to maintain his perch on the island week after week as he disposed, one by one, of anyone who might later prove to be a dangerous rival. Alert to the motivations and foibles of the other contestants, Rich stayed flexible and adaptable to the end, winning by the slimmest of margins, but winning nonetheless.

MOST CONTESTANTS HAD NO CLEAR GOAL

Interviewed afterward, most of the others admitted that they simply bumbled onto the island with only the foggiest notion of what the game was about. They said that their attention was initially diverted by the novelty and excitement of the situation, by the blossoming friendships, and by the activities of the camp. Many wanted to be nice and have people like them or convinced themselves that Machiavellian, duplicitous plots to kick others off the island were immoral. They muddled along trying to be friendly and/or useful and hoped that the game would work out in their favor. None had well-defined game plans for making it happen. They substituted passive "hopes" for an active pursuit of a practical and specific game plan.

As the group was whittled down and the $1,000,000 began to look more attainable, they all got with the program and began to lie, scheme, form "alliances" and play every bit as rough as Rich. It was "no more Mr. Nice Guy" all the way around. But the rest of the group had figured it out too late. So they lost to Rich, the one person who had zeroed in on the object of the game from the beginning.

An interesting question is how the vast majority of contestants managed to miss the point so completely and for so long? None of them were rich, so the acquisition of a $1,000,000 would be a life-changing event. Isn't this immensely more important than making a few new friends or having an adventure? If they got their hands on the money, they could buy all the friends and adventures they wanted. The rules were clearly delineated, the value of the prize was obvious, and the contestants were not, by any means, stupid. Why did it take them so long to get it? The overriding object of this game (and of most games, for that matter) is to win! Of course, the situation was new and exciting. Of course, there were new friendships to be made and camp activities to perform. But let's be honest, all of this pales in comparison with $1,000,000 in cash. What clouded these people's vision such that they forgot to focus on the $1,000,000 until it was too late?

FEAR OF FAILURE DIVERTED THEM FROM THEIR TRUE GOAL

As noted earlier, whenever you see maladaptive behavior, you should suspect that unconscious motivations, fear of failure and defense mechanisms, are active. How did they impact the situation here? In this case the members of the group saw that there were, after all, 15 other contestants. This made the odds against winning extremely high for any individual. The vast majority took these long odds to heart and felt themselves unlikely to win.

Remember the axiom that the harder you try to win, the more painful it is when you lose? It causes most people not to try their hardest when they fear that they will lose in any case. That came into play here. Subconsciously, most of the contestants shrunk back from pinning their hopes on the money because of the long odds. They did not want to risk the pain of failure by trying too hard to win when they felt they were so likely to lose.

It is similar to what happens to tennis players and other athletes who get behind in matches or games and tank. They also see the odds against them as too great to be worth risking an all-out effort, only, they suspect, to crash and burn in painful failure. They protect themselves from disappointment by quitting early. This same condition led most of the "Survivor One" contestants to put the concept of winning the $1,000,000 in the "hope-it-happens" compartment of their brains rather than the "demands-immediate-planning-and action" compartment. Fearing to build up hopes, only to have them dashed, they subconsciously made the decision to put off any serious and direct quest for the money until the odds were better. (Why get your hands dirty if you are so likely to lose anyway?) In the meantime, they avoided thinking too deeply about it, stayed friendly, tried to be useful, and waited to see more cards played. Subconscious fear of failure clouded their brains and diverted their attention toward activities that were less threatening.

Most of the contestants were simply behaving like normal people. Rich was the abnormal one—the one who will be good at winning in anything. This all became clear when the television viewing audience was polled and asked whether or not they would have employed Rich's scheming and manipulative methods had they been on the island. Half of the audience said they would not have done so. When Bryant Gumbel announced this result to the assembled "Survivor" contestants on the post-game show, one of them (Joel) clarified the situation when he piped up, "Oh sure. But guarantee them that they will win if they use Rich's methods, and 99 percent of them will do it." This was a dead giveaway that it was the long odds against winning that made most of the group shift their focus away from a clear and concrete plan to win the $1,000,000.

Rich, on the other hand, before he was even guaranteed a place on the island, actually told the producers of the show that he was going to win the $1,000,000. Unlike the others, he thought he was going to win in the first place, and this confidence, this minimal fear of failure, this "winners" mentality, cleared his mind and allowed him to zero in on his goal and on the best plan for achieving it. It helped him to keep his goal in mind throughout the competition and to only take actions that would help him achieve it. He made some wrong moves along the way, but saw them and corrected quickly.

GOALS AND YOUR GAME PLAN

Goals can be broken down into two categories: short-term and long-term. Your long-term goal is your major goal, the "pot of gold at the end of the rainbow," and is what you are ultimately trying to accomplish. Your short-term goals are stepping-stone achievements on the way to your long-term goal. They are simple, bite-sized objectives that lead you toward your ultimate objective. Effective achievement requires both types of goals, although, as we will discuss later, the short-term ones are the most important.

Equally essential is a game plan. This gives you the road map of your pathway to your long-term or ultimate goal and allows you to identify your short-term goals. All goals should be clearly identified (as specifically as possible) so you can keep your eye on them and not become scattered and disoriented. It is also preferable, though not always possible, for their attainments to, in some way, be measurable. Vague goals or goals that are, for all practical purposes, unattainable are only modestly helpful. Examples are goals like "getting rich" or "running a huge company." These are more in the "hope" than "goal" category. On the other hand, even vague goals or "pie in the sky" goals are better than none at all.

In this case, Rich's long-term goal was to win the $1,000,000—clear, simple and measurable. Next he constructed his game plan—form an alliance with the most trustworthy of his fellow competitors, vote off all the others, while ingratiating himself with the group by providing useful services. This allowed him to construct his short-term goals and assess priorities. His first short-term goal was to determine which of the others were the most trustworthy. Making a quick study, he settled on three candidates—Rudy, Susan, and Kelly. His next short-term goal was to gain their confidence and commit them to his alliance. Once this was accomplished, he systematically and step-by-step established and accomplished the other short-term goals to carry out his plan.

MODIFY SHORT-TERM GOALS THAT ARE NOT TAKING YOU WHERE YOU WANT TO GO

Some of his original short-term goals had to be modified because they didn't work. For example, as a corporate trainer, Rich initially tried to make himself useful to the group by using this experience to direct the group's activities. This seemed reasonable because when the group first arrived on the island, they were milling around on the beach without adequate food or shelter and with no coherent plan for obtaining them. They needed a leader. But as he tried to take control, Rich soon sensed that the others resented his approach as too "corporate." So he backed off. Later he became useful by supplying the group with fish, and this was appreciated. Rich was flexible, yet never lost sight of his ultimate goal. The result was victory.

The general formula for success is fivefold: (1) Clearly identify your ultimate goal. (2) Construct a game plan for reaching that goal. (3) Use this plan to set up short-term goals that lead towards your ultimate goal. They should be bite-sized, feasible, and, if possible, measurable. (4) Attack each of your short-term goals in order, one at a time, by focusing all your energies on it. Once it is accomplished, move on to attack your next short-term goal. (5) Monitor your overall progress toward your ultimate goal as more information becomes available. Consider whether or not you need to modify your game plan. If you modify the plan, change your short-term goals accordingly.

SETTING GOALS MAKES LARGE TASKS FEEL MANAGABLE

This goal-setting strategy works in any area, even one as mundane as school homework. My older son, Evan, was assigned four books for summer reading last year. Two and a half months of freedom seemed to be more than enough time to get the work done. But time was dissipated on a family vacation to Europe and in participating in a summer basketball league. With only a month of summer remaining and the better part of the four hefty volumes yet to be consumed, Evan looked at the pile of work in front of him and suddenly felt overwhelmed and panicky. He didn't know what to do first.

This is where a goal and game plan act like a raft in a stormy sea. Evan took a step backward and assessed the situation. To finish his reading assignment in the remaining time was his obvious long-term goal, and he needed a practical game plan to accomplish it. Evan added up the total number of pages to be read and divided by the number of days remaining before school started, yielding the number of pages he would have to read each day. His short-term goal was simply to finish his daily quota of pages. Stick to the plan day-by-day and ultimate success would be guaranteed. Here, by creating a plan with straightforward, achievable, short-term goals, Evan took control of the process and made the gross task feel less daunting.

EFFECTIVENESS REQUIRES FOCUS ON SHORT-TERM GOALS

Some years ago I was hired to consult with a racecar driver (whom I will call Steve). Steve drove oval tracks and had had great success early in his career but was now floundering. With a bit of digging, I learned that his main problem occurred when he fell behind. At this point Steve seemed to lose coordination, his lap times increased, and he was unable to catch up. The central question boiled down to, "Why did his lap times go up when he got behind?"

The answer lay in Steve's field of view. When he got behind, his concern about catching up directed his attention too far ahead on the track. He became overly aware of the leaders and of the ground he needed to make up. It hurt his coordination. Improvement came when he learned to ignore the leaders and forget about catching up. Steve drove best when he focused his full attention only on the track in front of him and only at an optimal distance ahead. Then he stayed relaxed, maintained his coordination, and was able to develop maximum speed.

Adopting this narrower point of focus did not stop Steve from knowing, in the back of his mind, that he needed to catch the leaders (which, of course, was his ultimate goal). But it would have been counter-productive to focus on it. On a moment-to-moment basis, it was best to confine all of his attention to his short-term goal of driving the car, as best he could, down the limited stretch of track immediately in front of him. He had to (please excuse the pun) focus on where the rubber meets the road. His long-term goal would be met simply by doing a good job on a succession of his short-term goals. Like chopping down a tree, all you have to focus on is each stroke of the axe. Accomplish this well and the tree will fall.

POORLY CHANNELED LONG-TERM GOALS CAN EVEN BE COUNTER-PRODUCTIVE

I once worked with a talented young college tennis player (let's call him Paul) whose long-term goals actually hindered his tennis development. How is this possible? Here is the story—you can judge for yourself.

Paul entered university as the second ranked junior in the United States. He was very talented and had already notched wins over several ranking players on the ATP (professional) tennis tour. Since his long term goal was to make his living competing on the ATP tour, Paul had debated, before entering university, whether he should turn professional immediately after graduating high school or accept one of the many full scholarships that had been offered. He decided to let the summer tournaments be his guide. If his results were good, he would turn pro, if not, he would go to college. A mediocre summer, though disappointing, made his decision easy—he went to college.

Chapter Six

The coach started Paul at the number one position on the team, but, still suffering disappointment from his lackluster summer, he had mixed results. On top of this, he was having difficulty adjusting to the team situation, where practices were disciplined and controlled by the coach, team mates were an ever-present factor—impacting his position on the team as well as his social and personal life, and pressure to make grades and maintain eligibility was constant. Before long, the coach moved Paul down to the number two position, where he played even worse, feeling that he was going backwards instead of forwards, and that his pro chances were receding. Additional losses got Paul moved down to the number three position. Here he found himself having increasing difficulty trying 100 percent against opponents who he considered to be well below his standard.

In fact, the whole college situation was becoming decidedly negative. It was depressing and constrictive. He felt the coach was unfair, because when players above him lost, the coach did not move Paul up, though he was ready enough to move Paul down when he lost. Practices were unproductive, and Paul did not feel like putting out strong efforts. Teammates got on his nerves, and to top it all off, when he played important matches in tournaments and had chances for big wins, he was becoming unusually tentative and losing. His world was falling apart, and his professional prospects seemed to be disintegrating.

After hearing Paul's tales of woe, it was clear to me that Paul had created for himself a poisonous stew. He had mixed a potpourri of interacting events into a confusing jumble that made him lose his way. It was my job to understand the underlying cause of the problems in order to simplify and clarify the situation. As it stood, Paul was bewildered and acting emotionally and counterproductively.

In unraveling the sequence of events, it was clear that the problems had started in the summer, when Paul disappointed himself by performing below expectation and dashing his hopes (or fantasies) of making a direct jump into the pros. Of course, his long-term goal was to play as a professional, but he was focusing on this prematurely. The jump was simply greater than his present abilities could support. And since Paul's development had always been smoothly upward (he had been ranked at the top of every junior division), he was thrown off balance by this unaccustomed failure. Self-doubt raised its ugly head. The lurking fear that he might not, after all, be able to make it as a pro arose and was suppressed. Like whistling in the dark, Paul convinced himself

82

that college tennis was merely a short interlude preceding his professional career. In so doing, he had entered college with the wrong attitude—he thought he was slumming.

Unprepared to concentrate 100 percent in matches and in practice, Paul was bound to be beaten often. And since losses erode confidence, he embarked on a downward spiral. Blaming the coach, teammates, and the school situation simply muddied up the waters. The ultimate solution involved gaining better perspective on how to reach goals.

Paul needed to turn his focus away from his long-term goal and towards practical short-term ones. As with all sports, reaching one's potential in tennis involves repetitive motor learning in practice in order to develop proper habits and techniques and then learning to use these habits and techniques through experience in competition. I suggested to Paul that all he needed to worry about were short-term goals such as devoting himself everyday in every practice to improving some part of his game and trying his best to win every competitive match. If he did this, his long-term goals would take care of themselves. I further pointed out that worrying about his position on the team or what his teammates were saying was a counter-productive, self-defeating distraction, heightened by uncertainty (fear) over his potential to become a successful pro. His only tennis concern need be to improve his skill as a player. That done, he would get whatever rewards his skills could justify.

In general, the key to meeting your long-term goals is to successfully meet your short-term goals. That is why I earlier stated that short-term goals are the key goals. As a magnifying glass focuses the sun's rays on a point, thus concentrating its heat and power, so your mind becomes more potent and effective when its full attention is focused on the goal at hand. Attending to distant goals on a moment-to-moment basis dissipates your mental force. Of course, you never totally forget about your long-term goals, and they remain in the back of your mind, but you just don't focus on them all the time.

Long-term goals supply overall direction and motivation. They function best if you bring them to the forefront at the beginning of a project, when they allow you to set up a viable game plan and an achievable set of short-term goals, and periodically thereafter so that you can maintain your bearings and make sure that your game plan continues to carry you in the right direction. The rest of your time should be devoted to doggedly pursuing your short-term goals with all the strength you can muster.

FOCUSING ON SHORT-TERM GOALS IS EFFECTIVE IN TENNIS COMPETITION

Champions win tennis matches by using this strategy. Their long-term goal is so obvious that they don't have to think much about it beforehand—to win the match. They construct a game plan that, ideally, uses their own strengths to attack their opponents' weaknesses. This gives them the best chance of winning the match. Their short-term goal becomes to win each point by using their game plan, and they focus all their mental, emotional, and physical resources on winning these points—one at a time. They don't have to concern themselves about winning the match. (In fact, they often make conscious efforts to avoid focusing on winning the match during play since it tends to make them nervous and is, therefore, counterproductive.) As long as they are sufficiently adept at attaining their short-term goals (winning points) their long-term goal will follow as a matter of course.

THIS STRATEGY WORKS IN ALL AREAS

Even a weight loss program becomes user-friendlier employing this strategy. Take, for example, Josh, who is finally determined to lose the extra 40 pounds he has put on in recent years. Now 62 years old, Josh has been consistently gaining weight despite cutting back on desserts and other fatty and sugary foods, a strategy that always worked for him when he was younger. Now it doesn't. Josh has realized that, as is the case with most people his age, a new set of circumstances has come into play that is causing him to pack on hard-to-lose pounds. First, with age his metabolism has slowed so that the calories needed to maintain his weight have diminished. His maintenance calories used to be 2,500 per day; now they are 2,000. Second, he has more aches and pains than before, so that spending his weekends playing basketball or tennis or going on marathon bike rides is no longer attractive. His older body is more inclined to head for the couch and the television than the track or sport's court. Thus, his ability to burn off massive amounts of calories in a hurry is gone. Finally, as his other pleasures have diminished with age, so the pleasures of the table have grown in importance. He tends to look forward to meals more, linger at the table longer, and eat larger portions. Simply cutting back on a few desserts and fatty foods is no longer enough.

A recent article in a health magazine has alarmed Josh about the dangers attendant to his swelling girth. He feels he has few enough good years left without reducing them by toting around superfluous abdominal flab. That fear and the embarrassment of exposing his white, jiggling midsection to public scrutiny at

84

the beach in the coming summer have elicited his vow to get serious about losing weight.

First he establishes his long-term goal of losing 40 pounds, a potentially overwhelming and depressing prospect that his strategy will, somehow, have to make more palatable. To this end he develops an intelligent game plan. Josh calculates that with maintenance calories of 2,000 per day and a walking program averaging three miles per day, he will burn a total of about 2,300 calories per day. He works out daily menus whereby he takes in 1,800 calories a day, an amount that gives him leeway to enjoy his meals and not feel deprived. This means that he will burn off 500 calories a day of stored fat. Since a pound of fat will be burned off for each 3,500 calories, he will lose a pound a week. Burning an excess of 500 calories per day is a manageable short-term goal. If Josh does not dwell on the 40 pounds he has to lose, but merely focuses on meeting his daily goal, the big loss will ultimately take care of itself. Josh mustn't be in a hurry to accomplish his long-term goal. He uses it only to set up his game plan and short-term goals. Then he has only to stick with his game plan for the required months, and his long-term goal will fall into his lap.

SUMMARY

You will be happiest when you are improving in some way and moving toward a goal. This is best accomplished by setting up a clear long-term goal, a game plan for reaching it, a series of short-term goals, and then devoting all your powers to meeting your short-term goals. You can trot out your long-term goal from time to time for motivation and to see if you are progressing towards it as planned, but never forget to keep focused on meeting short-term goals.

Before and during the process you should clearly identify and, figuratively, set on the table in front of you, your fears of failure. Do you think you are not smart enough, not educated enough, an inept athlete, lacking in willpower, have never done it before, not a "winner" type, and so forth? Consciously recognize that you can overcome any of these supposed weaknesses with sufficient effort and purpose. If you find yourself procrastinating or are losing your resolve during the achievement process, trot out these fears again. They are, behind the scenes, disorienting you. Bring them out into the open, vow to overpower them, and immediately start moving forward. Success reduces fears of failure and breeds success.

KEEPING GOALS IN MIND

The champions never take actions that lead them away from their goals.

T he champions never forget where their best interests lie. (This could be considered as a corollary to the last chapter on goal setting, but it is worthy of a separate chapter because so few people can keep their basic objectives in mind throughout the achievement process.) While, as discussed in Chapter 6, the winners do not consciously focus on their ultimate goals at all times, they never lose track, at some lower level of consciousness, of what they are trying to accomplish—the object of the game, so to speak. The losers, by contrast, often seem mindless of their own best interests. The champions rarely do anything that does not help them win, while the losers often do, a tendency, as usual, driven by the fear of failure. In fact, the "Golden Rule" for anyone working towards a goal is to test any action before taking it with the question, "WILL THIS HELP ME GET WHAT I WANT?" If the answer is not yes, don't do it.

A truly bizarre example of what can happen when one does not apply this test was provided by Jeff Tarango, a 26-year-old American, at Wimbledon in 1996. Tarango had never before won a match at Wimbledon. But this year he was in the third round and had an excellent chance of getting to the round of 16 because he was playing Alexander Mronz of Germany, whose name in the tennis world is hardly a household (or for that matter, pronounceable) word. During the course of the match, Tarango hit what he thought was an ace, but it was called a fault. After fruitlessly trying to convince the umpire to overrule the linesman, Tarango was heckled by the crowd as he walked into position for his second serve. Angrily he told them to "Shut up." The umpire gave him a code violation for "audible obscenity." Although it only amounted to a warning, this so infuriated Tarango that he demanded that the referee supervisor come to the court. The supervisor dutifully did so and told Tarango to continue playing. Tarango then called the umpire "the most corrupt official in the game" and was promptly assessed a point penalty for verbal abuse which cost him the game. At this Tarango shouted "That's it. No way. That's it." He picked up his bags, stalked off the court, and entered the history books as the first player in the Open era to default himself at Wimbledon. To make matters worse (yes, it's always possible), Tarango held a press conference at which he justified calling the umpire "corrupt" by accusing him, on the basis of hearsay, of having, in the past, "given" matches to players who were his friends.

Now let's tote up the damages. Tarango threw away an excellent chance to advance in the tournament since he was, after all, favored in the match. He was defaulted in his mixed doubles, which did not endear him to his partner. It cost him a lot of money which he could ill afford since he is not one of the stars of the game—fines totaling approximately $50,000, not counting legal expenses, as well as any additional prize money he might have won. Finally, his public image was not enhanced by making himself look like an overgrown brat who would have been well served by a few good spankings as a child. All in all it was not one of Tarango's better afternoons, the object of the game (to win the match) having apparently slipped his mind.

With all these damages accruing as a result of his actions, one might reasonably wonder how a man of Tarango's substantial intellect (he is also a likeble, funny, bright Stanford man and a friend of mine) could have so completely lost track of his simple goal of winning the match? The answer is fear of failure (he was losing), exacerbated by the stress and emotion of the situation, drove his actions. He was afraid that he was going to lose the match, and this fanned the flames of his irrationality. Quitting was his unconscious way of escaping from a situation that he feared would end badly. If you don't believe this, picture the following thought experiment: God appears over Tarango's shoulder and whispers in his ear that he is guaranteed to win the match. Now what would Tarango have done? He might still have fought with the umpire, but I would bet a lot of money that he would have stuck around to win the match.

THE CHAMPIONS ARE DIFFERENT

John McEnroe had a similar fiery temperament, but his situational judgment was not driven by fear. Because he thought he was going to win, he was able to comprehend where the line demarcating disaster was and exert enough self-control (although it didn't look like it) to avoid crossing it. He got into emotional twits where he made unreasonable demands, berated linesmen and umpires, and threw matches into confusion, but he usually benefited from this behavior. His behavior intimidated linesmen into giving him the benefit of the doubt on close calls; it disturbed his opponents and put off their games; and McEnroe stimulated himself with adrenaline and often played better.

One year he did manage to get himself defaulted in the Australian Open, but he said after the match that he had been unaware of a recent rule change where the authorities had cut down by one the number of abuses a player was allowed before default. The progression toward default had formerly been "warning," "point penalty," "game penalty," "DEFAULT," but this had been changed to "warning," "point penalty," "DEFAULT." McEnroe simply miscalculated and thought he could afford one more penalty. In contrast with Tarango, McEnroe may sometimes have looked like an uncontrolled, irrational wild man, but all the while he was carefully counting his penalties so that he could stop himself before he went too far. McEnroe didn't often forget where his interests lie.

THE WINNERS MUST DO IT IN BUSINESS TOO

It is usually easier to remain cognizant of one's goals in business than it is in sports, though the unsuccessful manage to lose their way in either arena. The cause of the dislocation in both cases is destructive emotion (usually fear of failure) that overpowers logic and causes people to lose track of the object of the game. The emotions in competitive sports are usually closer to the surface and more intense than they are in business, so they pose a more constant and potentially overwhelming threat. Nonetheless, there are plenty of counterproductive emotions lurking in business too, and the successful businessperson, like the successful athlete, must continually be on the alert for them.

I was reminded of this fact during a consulting session with a bright young lady (let's call her Deborah) who was having difficulty in her new job. The heart of her problem was that her insecurities and fears were clouding her vision and causing her to lose sight of her goals. But I am getting ahead of the story, so let's backup.

Deborah's background is unremarkable, but her talents and personal qualities are exceptional. Although she lacks a college education, Deborah is attractive, tasteful in her dress, carries herself well, speaks with intelligence and convic-

89

tion, and, in sum, presents herself in a high-class, competent manner. In addition, she is a reliable finisher. When Deborah is given a task, she gets it done. When she has an appointment, she shows up early, and when she says she will do something, she does it. Although she has always held down an outside job, Deborah is a wonderful mother to her two teenaged children and manages her household with uncommon skill and efficiency. Dinner is always beautifully prepared and on time, the closets and drawers are neat and organized, and the floors, carpets, and countertops have that recently scrubbed, spotless look. How she keeps everything so together while working is a marvel to her friends.

Yet Deborah needs to work. Although her husband makes a reasonable salary, it alone is not enough to enable the family to live in the nicer part of town, send the two children to private religious school, and enjoy the clothes, possessions, and entertainments of upper-middle class urban life. So Deborah has always pitched in, managing, over the years, to earn a high hourly wage at part-time jobs like selling clothes at Nordstroms, or working as a hairdresser, although neither these nor any of her other jobs have been truly satisfying.

But the new job appeared to be different. Deborah was hired by one of the most talented, respected, and highly paid interior decorators in the San Francisco area to work as her assistant. It seemed to be a stroke of luck. This was Deborah's element. She has excellent taste and loves beautiful things. (In fact, she is a natural born shopper, lacking only unlimited funds to make a full-time occupation of it for her own account.) Unfortunately, Deborah was not hired to do the decorating, but rather as a one-person office administrator and general "get it done" person. Nonetheless, she would learn the decorating business from one of the best people in the industry and might, in time, be able to play a more creative role in her boss's business or strike out on her own and decorate for her own clients. Either way, the future appeared to be loaded with potential, and, best of all, Deborah was being well paid while she learned.

In addition, the job had other unique benefits that melded in well with Deborah's powerful family orientation. The office was located near her home so Deborah's drive time to work was nil, and she could get home quickly if necessary. Her daily hours ended early enough so she could be on hand to greet her children when they returned from school. Fridays were off so she was free to spend the day readying the house for the weekend and preparing for the Sabbath meal, which is so important to her religious, Jewish family. It was hard to imagine a job more suitable to Deborah's needs, except for one problem—she was so unhappy with the work that each day she came home emotionally distraught, often in tears. By the time I saw her, Deborah had been at the job for four months and was barely hanging on. Benefits and opportunities be damned, she wanted to quit.

What was getting to her? First, Deborah told me that she was completely out of place doing administrative work. Her other jobs had involved sales and fashion. She had no previous experience with the computers, paperwork, bookkeeping or the other tools employed in office administration. She was having great difficulty learning these strange new skills and felt totally out of her element. To make matters worse, her boss was a temperamental perfectionist, difficult to please. and quick to criticize. If Deborah made mistakes, her boss became irritated. Her cutting remarks hurt Deborah deeply, and even though the boss would later become remorseful and apologize, Deborah was beset with uncertainty, constantly fearing that she was about to be fired. Each afternoon Deborah came home in a nervous funk, hating the work and dreading the morrow's mistakes and reproaches.

In telling me her story, Deborah concluded by saying that life is too short to be miserable in one's job, a notion that struck me as eminently reasonable. My first impulse was to agree with her and suggest that she find another job, one more closely attuned to her talents and temperament. But when I analyzed the situation more thoroughly, I came to a startlingly different conclusion.

Despite her many talents and strong personal qualities, Deborah was deeply insecure. Whether the origin of her fears was genetic, or whether they were caused by her single parent, love-deprived childhood and exacerbated by her lack of education, no one can be sure. But these fears of failure were a major contributor to her problems and unhappiness. They were causing her to become emotional, irrational, and to lose sight of her practical goals.

First, her primary goal was to make the money that her family needed. The new job was providing that and promised to provide much more of it in the future. Deborah was preparing to throw this away, claiming that her problem was one of temperamental unsuitability for administrative work. But that is not really true. In fact, administrative work suits Deborah's mentality quite well. She is organized, detail-oriented, and a perfectionist (anyone can see this by looking at her impeccably organized house)—ideal traits for running a small office. Her real difficulty is that she lacks the specific administrative skills to run this particular office, and she is afraid that she cannot learn them.

Deborah was trying to learn an Excel computer program and light bookkeeping but was not catching on quickly. Her lack of formal education made her insecure and fearful. She suspected that there were vast areas of technical information and skill that everyone else had but that she did not. When her boss asked her if she knew how to type a particular kind of business letter or if she knew what to do with a vender invoice, Deborah answered "no" and felt stupid. Then the fear set in, her mind went into "panic" mode, and in this state it took her twice as long to learn anything as it should. All of this was intensified by the boss' caustic scrutiny. The situation was tailor-made to be unpleasant. Here is an insecure person, thrust into a new job for which she is untrained, and all the while she is being judged and criticized by her vexatious boss. No wonder her every nerve fiber cried out to quit and escape.

But making decisions based on emotion is generally bad policy. My advice to Deborah was that she change her attitude and keep her priorities firmly in mind. I suggested that she stop convincing herself that administrative work was beyond her capabilities. Such an appearance was only temporary and was exacerbated by her fears of failure. Once she became familiar and comfortable with the necessary tools (which are simpler than she imagines), I could almost guarantee that she would become an excellent administrator. At that stage her uncertainty and fears would disappear. She also needed to dispose of the notion that the job was supposed to be fun right away. She had to realize that this was a time for learning new skills, not fun. She had to view her present development as attending graduate school or going to boot camp—as a means to an end rather than as an end in itself. She had to realize that she was an apprentice, not a master craftsperson. That could only come later.

And so what if, in the meantime, she had a tough boss? The boss owned the ball, and if Deborah wanted to play the game, she had to accept that the boss had every right to make the rules. She had to turn her mind around so that she could follow them happily and be grateful for her opportunities rather than bemoaning the fact that the boss behaved in a manner she found unattractive. Members of athletic teams often have difficult and opinionated coaches. The losers fight their coaches and resent them. Their performances deteriorate, and they blame their coaches. The winners accept the fact that their coaches have the ultimate power. They extract the good and do their best to ignore the bad, all the while focusing on improving their own performances. They make the team and the others sit on the bench or quit. I had some nasty professors when I was in grad school, and marine recruits must survive rough drill instructors. We all live through it and, hopefully, become better and more competent people as a result of the experiences. Deborah's fun would come after she had paid her dues. It would come when she had become proficient at her job and more valuable. It would come when she earned a bigger paycheck than she had ever before thought possible.

Quitting so quickly would relegate her to the same low paying, unsatisfying job pool that she had been in for most of her adult life. Of course, she might then stumble into some other great new job, but at 43 years of age, how much more time could she afford to spend looking and hoping? And even then she would still have to learn new skills. Insecurities would still have to be faced and overcome. There was no easy way out.

With counseling Deborah was ultimately able to see past her fears and realize that insecurities had clouded her judgment. She had forgotten her objectives. She returned to work with a clearer vision of her long-term goals. With these in front of her, her attitude changed. She focused on her immediate objectives of learning new skills and assumed for the time being, that she would eventually be able to handle the job. Her stress level receded. She focused on appreciating her good fortune rather than exaggerating her tribulations, and this helped her become less emotionally troubled. The job became more pleasant and her learning progressed more easily than she ever imagined. Four months later, Deborah was on top of her job, her comfort level had increased, and her boss was so pleased that she even awarded Deborah a small bonus.

Whether or not Deborah will choose to remain in her job on a long-term basis is still a question in my mind. She may still ultimately dislike the work or her boss. But having mastered the mechanics of the job and, therefore, lost most of her fear and emotionalism, Deborah can keep her goals in mind and make that decision more rationally.

LEO WYLER TEACHES ME TO BE PRACTICAL

Early in my career Leo Wyler, founder of TRE Corp. (a company that was listed on the New York Stock Exchange and ultimately acquired by Alcoa), gave me a good example of mature business thinking. At the time I was managing a small private investment company for which Leo had supplied the capital. An associate of Leo's had behaved with questionable morality in a matter that ended up costing Leo a lot of money. Essentially, Leo found out that he had been screwed. But he never said a word about it. When he talked to the guy, Leo was as friendly as ever and carried on their business relationship as if nothing had happened. The other man had no inkling that Leo was aware of his misdeeds. This struck me as odd, and I asked Leo why he didn't lay into the sneaky SOB, tell him off, and refuse to ever do business with him again.

Leo's explanation was that the business world is small. He said that although he doesn't need the guy now, things could very well change in the future. In fact, this fellow might some day end up in a position where his good will would be vital to Leo's interests. What if he were the only person that could help Leo in some future situation? If he knew how Leo felt, he would end up hating Leo, he would be wary of Leo, and Leo would never be able to do business with him again. Leo said it would be foolhardy to foreclose his future options simply for the momentary satisfaction of venting his spleen. Besides, Leo was no longer in any danger from the man because Leo now knew what he was dealing with and would, in his future dealings with the fellow, be watchful and protect himself.

At the same time, Leo had no intention of giving up the option of retribution. But telling someone off and getting retribution are two different things. Leo intended to hurt the man in the future if the opportunity arose. And this would be so much the easier if the man thought Leo was friendly. If Leo ultimately decided to act, it would only be when he was sure that he would never need the man again and only when he could inflict apt retribution. (A five-minute tongue-lashing hardly qualifies.) Leo was never in a hurry to act emotionally and was content to keep his thoughts to himself indefinitely. His priorities were always clear—business interests came first and emotional satisfaction was a distant second.

DICK GOULD DOES IT AT STANFORD

Dick Gould is the most successful college tennis coach in history, his teams having won the NCAA Championships 18 times (as of 2001). Yet before Gould arrived, Stanford had no substantial tennis reputation nor was Gould anything more than a mediocre tennis player himself. Yet he was able to attract, coach and control world-class talents such as John McEnroe, Roscoe Tanner, Sandy and Gene Mayer, Tim Mayotte (all top 10 in the world), and others. What were his secrets?

One of them is that he never loses sight of his objectives. One afternoon I was visiting Gould at Stanford and watching the team practice. On one court hitting was a former team member of Gould's, let's call him Steve, who had stopped by Stanford to get a workout. I remembered Steve as a querulous and self-centered fellow, and it was well known among the coaches that he had given Gould nothing but grief over the years. Yes, Steve was a fine physical talent, but he had disrupted many team practices by insisting on having his own practice needs met, regardless of his teammates, and he had often put forth half-hearted efforts in team matches. He would have been the kind of guy that, after he graduated, I would have been happy to never see again. It would have been hard for me to fake it and make him feel welcome.

I am sure Gould felt the same way, but you would never have known it. Gould realized that the tennis world is small. Steve knows a lot of people, and Gould might need his help some day to convince a talented recruit to come to Stanford. In any case, Gould knows that he can't possibly do himself any good by letting Steve know that he doesn't like him. So Steve was never going to know. Gould was his usual friendly, charming self, and after practice, Steve went off with those nice, warm, fuzzy feelings that you get when you have been in homey surroundings and feel welcome. And Gould had another ally whom he could call upon for help if needs be. Gould never lets his feelings jeopardize his interests.

FORGETTING YOUR GOALS IS NOT SMART IN INTERPERSONAL RELATIONS EITHER

Wise people remember their goals in social situations as well. During conversations with others, they may not overtly ask themselves the crucial question—"Is this conversation achieving the purposes I wish?"—but they keep it subconsciously in mind nonetheless. On the other hand, many people do not.

One negative example is that of Charlie, an obnoxious but moderately successful businessman. Charlie likes to talk about himself and particularly about his business successes. He verbally preens as he describes his adept judgment in the stock market or how much money he made in a recent deal. He is very intense and likes to get exceptionally close as he talks, right in his listener's face. In this way, he assures himself of his listener's undivided attention. As he continues patting himself on the back, the listener develops the growing impulse to run.

The first question we might ask is, "What is Charlie attempting to achieve with these tactics?" The answer, of course, is that Charlie wants his listener to think well of him. He is trying to impress his listener and look good. But Charlie has never consciously thought about his approach. He is just mindlessly acting upon his emotional drive to fluff up his own feathers. And, in so doing, he is, of course, achieving exactly the opposite of what he intends. His listener is inclined to dislike him, to avoid him in the future, and to wish him ill in his business dealings. Charlie would have been better off staying home from the party. Instead, he spent an hour of his valuable time creating an enemy.

If Charlie had, for an instant, considered his goals, he would have known that his approach was taking him in the wrong direction. He should have thought back to his own reactions to people like himself—people whose insecurities and egos are hanging out and whose involvements are primarily with themselves—and he could have predicted the impression he would make. But Charlie, like so many people in social situations, simply forgot about his true interests and let his emotional impulses run wild. The wise person remembers his goals, stays alert to his listener, and keeps a lid on his emotions. (See Appendix 5 for simple rules to help make a conversation interesting.)

SUMMARY

Regardless of the arena in which you contemplate action—be it in your job, dealing with your spouse, interpersonally, or in sports—always be sure that these actions lead you toward and not away from your goals.

THE
FEELING
OF CONTROL

The champions feel that they can
control the outcome of events.

High achievers possess a characteristic termed by psychologists as an "internal locus of control." If we throw out the big words and translate this into English, it means that champions feel they can personally control the outcome of events. This feeling empowers them. They believe that their own efforts will ultimately produce results, and they feel responsible for success or failure.

This is in contrast to the less effective person who has an "external locus of control." These people believe that the outcome of events is determined by factors beyond their control—by other individuals, society as a whole, the government, their employers, or just luck. Why? Because fear of failure impels them to dodge responsibility. Their insecurities delude them into believing their own excuses, and, attributing failure to factors other than themselves, they learn little from their losses. So they lose more often than they should. Fearing that they will lose, these people try to avoid the pain of that loss by shirking responsibility for it.

Does this mean that the champions are so irrational as to really think that everything is under their control? Certainly not. They are well aware that good and ill-fortune exist. They have had ample empirical proof of it because they have lost in the past, so they would not bet their lives on the outcome of any particular contest. But the crucial distinction is that they act as if they had this control. In their cores, they are self-reliant. They unconsciously assume that they have the power to force a win if they apply sufficient effort, even though they know rationally that there is risk of loss. It is somewhat schizophrenic in

97

that these two conflicting ideas co-exist at different levels of consciousness. At the conscious level, they know they could lose, but at the unconscious level, they feel they will win.

A corollary belief of the champions is that losing is their fault. This makes losses hurt more, but it also motivates them to try harder as well as to analyze their performances afterward for mistakes or weaknesses. They mentally rehash their actions to figure out what they did wrong. Once they have zoned in on their mistakes and weaknesses, they can work intelligently to improve and can avoid making the same mistakes again.

HOW DO WE MEASURE IT?

Psychologists use a "ring toss" game to differentiate individuals with an "internal locus of control" from those with an "external locus of control." The game's objective is to see how many rings out of ten a subject can toss over a peg at a distance. The experimenter allows the subject to choose the distance. They have found that the people with an "internal locus of control" choose a reasonable but challenging distance. They choose a distance where their efforts can be effective. The people with an "external locus of control" tend to choose distances that are either so close that they can hardly miss or so far that success is a matter of chance only—thus reducing the risk that their efforts will be the cause of any failure.

One former member of my Pepperdine team, lets call him Jeff, exemplified the "external locus of control" mentality. Jeff appeared to have everything going for him. He came from a wealthy family, had great physical talent, and was good-looking, bright, well spoken, and extremely successful with the ladies. Unfortunately for him, he was also extremely insecure.

This led to his becoming unpopular with his teammates. He was self-centered, shallow, and critical of others. Appearances were overly important to Jeff, and he was quick to blame anyone but himself for his problems. On the tennis court he had a tendency to choke under pressure, yet he could not squarely face this and take steps to counter it. He preferred to fake it and pretend that he did not choke.

In a broad sense, tennis is a game of controlled risk. The successful players take the minimum risk necessary to accomplish their objectives. Along these lines, they know their own limitations and virtually never hit the ball so hard that it is out of control, sensing that in doing so the percentages are against them. Bystanders may think it is courageous to whack the ball and go for a big shot in important situations, but champions don't do it unless they have a legitimate core feeling that they will MAKE THE SHOT. The less successful, on the other hand, will insist on forcing the big shot, even when they are fearful and lack confidence in the shot. Consequently, they will usually miss and lose. Hitting hard and hoping the ball will go in is a formula for disaster in tennis. It is like playing the ring toss game and throwing the ring from across the street. In tennis the winning players don't hope. They control the ball and hit shots that they feel they can routinely make.

As you might imagine, Jeff used to go for big shots in the important situations. And as you also might imagine, he used to miss them. That was bad enough, but it was even less helpful when he urged his teammates to do the same thing.

In one big match against a rival school, the score was tied at four matches all. The deciding match was being played, and the members of both teams were crowded along the sidelines, verbally driving their teammate on. The tension grew as the match progressed deep into the third set. Finally, our guy reached match point by getting an ad on his opponent's serve. Our guy needed a good serve return but that would not be easy since the opponent had a nasty serve and the pressure of the situation made hitting any shot difficult.

In these circumstances, my usual advice is to take a deep breath, pick a spot for your return, focus on the ball, and play the point as routinely as possible. Since your opponent is under as much pressure as you are, you need to avoid trying a wild, panicky shot. This usually results in a quick error and lets your opponent off the hook without having to play. But the advice Jeff shouted out to his teammate exemplified the loser's mentality. "Take a chance. Go for it!" he yelled. He was speaking for himself and was endorsing the old "hit and hope" strategy. Jeff had put into words what I had sensed about him all along, which was his desire to give up responsibility for outcomes. Not trusting in his own ability to perform (but pretending that he did), Jeff was only too happy to put his fate in the hands of the Gods—and remove it from his own.

If Jeff could have acknowledged his own fears and insecurities, he could have helped himself. He needed to face the fact that his nerves would not allow him to go for a big shot in certain high-pressure situations. Realizing this, Jeff could have worked on relaxation and focusing techniques that would have allowed him to perform better. He could have attempted less demanding shots in these situations. Faking it and lying to himself only doomed him to endlessly repeat his original errors.

IN BUSINESS, THE
WINNERS ARE FINISHERS

A corollary to having an "internal locus of control" is the feeling of personal responsibility that the successful businesspeople have for getting things done. They are particularly aggressive and resourceful at overcoming obstacles because they believe that finishing tasks is within their power if they try hard enough. They understand that no one else is interested in excuses for their failure to complete a task. Finishing is what counts, and these people assume responsibility for making it happen.

On the other hand, the loser, with the "external locus of control," tends to become passive in the face of obstacles and is happy to leave the completion of tasks to others. These people are insecure and shrink back from the difficulties and pressures involved in finishing. When problems arise, they move on to other tasks, blaming their failures to finish the first task on other people or on circumstances beyond their control. Instead of performance, they provide excuses and humbug themselves into believing that excuses are adequate substitutes. The losers habitually skip from the carnage of one uncompleted task to another without so much as a backward look. As long as they stay busy, they convince themselves that a backlog of unfinished tasks and unkept promises is not their fault.

As usual, fear of failure is a prominent element in driving many individuals to procrastinate finishing tasks. A survey by Esther Rothblum and colleagues of 342 college students looked into the causes of procrastination in writing term papers. Almost 50 percent of the students told investigators that they were procrastinators, and the most common reason given was fear of failure.

Some years ago I was hired to consult for a high-end dress shop business owned equally by two partners. One (we'll call her Mary) was an energetic finisher, and the other (we'll call her Sally) couldn't seem to get out of her own way. Mary was a perfectionist and obsessed with meeting obligations and keeping her word. Sally, on the other hand, took on projects and abandoned them in midstream when they became difficult or made promises to customers and did not keep them. Mary was constantly scrambling to fill in the holes, and in the process, was becoming a nervous wreck.

The partners were both bright and well spoken; both worked long, hard hours; and both were talented in recognizing the latest fashions and merchandising them. Despite the difficulties caused by Sally's inability to finish, the business was extraordinarily successful. But Mary was about ready to kill Sally. Sally, on the other hand, appeared completely oblivious to any problems with Mary. When Mary complained, Sally looked at her as if she were hallucinating. She replied nonchalantly that if Mary thought there was a problem, then there must be a problem, never acknowledging that there actually were problems, let alone accepting any responsibility for them.

It did not take me long to conclude that the business itself was excellent and could continue to prosper as long as Mary was willing to work extraordinarily hard to pick up the pieces left by Sally's broken promises and partially completed projects. I did not believe that Sally was capable of changing because she refused to acknowledge her weaknesses. Moreover, as long as Mary continued to hold the business together, Sally didn't really have any problems—other than the risk that Mary would, one day, garrote her with a silk stocking or handy telephone cord.

The ultimate solution was to sell the business. This was unfortunate for both partners on an economic basis but was necessary on an emotional one. Because they were equal partners, Mary could never control Sally, nor could she get Sally out of the business. Sally liked coming to work, and it made her feel important to own a successful business. In her own mind she took much of the credit for building the business and would never consent to sell her share to Mary. Most disastrously, Sally would never own up to her own failings or take responsibility for them. This made it impossible for her to change and a stalemate ensued. Since Mary could not stand the stress and emotional turmoil of the status quo, the business had to go.

The lesson to be learned is that if you are considering a business partnership, make sure that your partner has an "internal locus of control" so that he or she gets things done. (Would it appear unseemly to ask them to do a ring-toss test before committing to the partnership?)

Taking responsibility is beneficial on a corporate as well as a personal basis. A Stanford Business School study found that corporations suffering a bad earnings year that publicly took responsibliity for their losses did better the following year than companies that blamed external factors for their problems. This is, of course, an obvious result since denying responsibility for problems is not a terribly helpful prelude to solving them.

DENYING RESPONSIBILITY FOR
FAILINGS IN ANY AREA IS DISASTEROUS

During the time I was writing this chapter, I happened to turn on the television and watch an episode of "48 Hours" with Dan Rather. The show was about compulsive gambling, and the central character was Melanie Morgan, a television journalist who had gained some small-time celebrity traveling to the world's hot spots for stories and hosting local television news shows. She was also a compulsive gambler who lost her job and almost lost her family because of it.

Melanie told a sad story of addiction. It started when she had a heartbreaking miscarriage that left her disturbed and depressed. In pain and vulnerable, she happened upon a poker club at a local bowling alley and started to play. She immediately found that she loved the action and the adrenaline rush that came with the game, and before long she was hooked. Melanie played constantly, dissipated the family savings, and ran up huge credit card bills. She went on all-night benders and, the next morning, staggered into the television station for her news show bleary-eyed and unprepared. Of course she soon lost her job.

During that time Melanie became pregnant again and had a healthy baby boy whom she adored. She wanted to be a good mother and was—when she was around. But too often she was at the poker parlor. During those times she left her young son with her teenaged stepson, who became resentful, had a short fuse, and eventually physically abused the child. In came the authorities, and her husband took the child and left. I could go on, but I think you get the general idea—she was making a hash of her life.

Melanie sought treatment for her "gambling addiction" at a clinic that worked with compulsive gamblers. The psychologist there talked about genetic predispositions and withdrawal symptoms, similar to those associated with alcoholism. She came out determined to kick the habit but relapsed.

Watching the "48 Hours" program, my take was different. Mine was that Melanie believed that her "gambling addiction" was triggered by her miscarriage and fueled by a genetic predisposition to gamble, neither of which were her "fault." She could not shake the gambling, although she made numerous half-hearted attempts, because she felt that the problem was imposed on her by factors outside of herself—the "external locus of control" issue again. This lessened her resolve.

As the program went on, I found myself becoming annoyed. The audience was induced to conclude, "What bad luck! Why if poor Melanie just hadn't had that miscarriage and wasn't genetically predisposed to gamble, her life would have been fine." "BALONEY!" was my take. I was irritated because psychologists today have a nasty tendency to label as addictions a wide variety of behaviors that used to simply be called weaknesses or character deficiencies. The difference is more than semantic. Addictions appear to be largely outside of the addict's control while character deficiencies or weaknesses are not. It's easier to say, "Poor me. I'm addicted." than it is to admit to a character weakness—and, worse still, to be personally responsible for changing it.

Nowadays, psychologists talk about "food addiction" or "sex addiction" as if they were equivalent to alcohol or drug addiction. I am just waiting for one of them to pop up on the "Oprah Show" and claim that some loser can't work because he or she is addicted to watching television on the couch in the afternoon and eating Cheetos. This is just "Dr. Feel Good's" way of subtly making excuses for patients and allowing them to deny personal responsibility for their failings. I am sure it's good for the psychology business because it's what the patients want to hear, but such talk weakens people.

HITTING BOTTOM MOTIVATES CHANGES

Near the end of the program Melanie told of how she finally cured herself. As happens so often in this kind of situation, Melanie had to hit bottom before she made the deep, heartfelt commitment to change her ways. The realization that she was about to irrevocably lose her husband, child, and everything else of value woke her up. All the talk about the reasons why she gambled only took her eye off the ball. The reasons why didn't matter. Excuses were not going to save her. The only thing that mattered was what she was going to do about it. She ultimately got the idea through her head that no one else could change her behavior except her, and if she didn't, she would be ruined. Staring at the abyss, she took responsibility for making personal changes and made them. The process is simple. Not easy, but simple.

SUMMARY

The people that take responsibility themselves—that take pains to control their own destinies and are willing to accept the consequences—be it in business, sports, or life, are the ones that win. Those that don't are lost. Strive to be among the former, not the latter.

A SOLUTION TO ANY PROBLEM

The champion assumes that there
is a solution for any problem.

This is not usually a conscious assumption, but it pervades the actions of the winners. No matter what the problem, they believe that if they look long enough and work hard enough, they will find its solution. In order to improve their performances, they follow a sequence of identifying problems, searching for their causes, and attempting solutions. If the first solution doesn't work, they try another. If this doesn't work, they try a third, and simply keep at it until the problem is solved. Then they go to work on the next problem and use the same approach until they solve it too. They remain motivated because their core belief that there is a solution for any problem is a hopeful one. They have the subconscious feeling that all will end up well, despite present difficulties, because they feel that a solution exists and that their quests are not, therefore, hopeless.

In contrast, the people who lack this core belief lose heart and give up if they cannot solve a problem quickly. They are insecure to begin with, and their unconscious fears of failure make them apprehensive about solving difficult problems. As a result, they dread problems and go to great lengths to avoid dealing with them. They cringe when their associates call to their attention problems that they are obligated to solve. They don't really want to know about problems (the "ostrich" approach), even though this information is a vital prelude to any necessary corrective action. When a problem manages to force itself upon them, only a few failed approaches are required to confirm their established belief that the problem is, for them, insurmountable. They bail out and direct their attention elsewhere.

Chapter Nine

MARTY LAURENDEAU FOOLED ME

The achievements of Marty Laurendeau, a former member of my Pepperdine tennis team, provide a good example of the winner's problem-solving attitude applied to athletics. Marty was a "walk on" at Pepperdine, which means that he was not good enough to get a tennis scholarship, so he had to pay his own way. He was a low ranking Canadian junior with a fair serve, no forehand, no volley, and no competitive skills. His assets were that he was tall, had a good backhand, and had started tennis late, so he was inexperienced. This gave me some hope that I could teach Marty how to play, but he was a real long shot.

Watching Marty compete was painful. He was very quiet and had a somewhat depressed look. Below the surface, hordes of insecurities simmered, waiting to erupt. Sometimes Marty would get ahead in a set and have a chance to win it. But he would tighten up and become tentative out of fear that he might blow his opportunity. Naturally, his fortunes would decline, and the set would begin to slip away. Suddenly Marty would fling his racket violently into the fence and scream, "It's happening again. I can never finish anybody off!"

In fact, he played so badly when he first arrived at Pepperdine that he was not able to even practice with the top players on the team. His skill level was so far below theirs that he could not even give them a decent game, so most days he and Kelly Moore, the only other player on the team that played at Marty's level, practiced together. What was not apparent, however, was that despite all his obvious shortcomings, Marty had a winner's mentality. He is an excellent example of the fact that one can have plenty of insecurities and fears of failure, yet still be a champion. In fact, we all have these fears. Our successes depend on how we deal with them.

Marty had the unusual ability to understand what his problems were and to systematically work on them over a long period of time. He started with his forehand. With my help Marty realized that he was not getting his weight into the shot and that was he using insufficient body rotation. Together we took the stroke apart and reconstructed it from scratch. It was a painstaking process, but Marty spent six months diligently developing the habits of taking the racquet back early and stepping forward into the shot.

YOU GET WORSE BEFORE YOU GET BETTER

Changing an old motor habit is difficult. You get worse at first because you are doing something different and suddenly having to think about an action that was previously automatic. This is disruptive and causes you to make mistakes.

Eventually, if you are sufficiently disciplined and can stick with the process through all the frustration, the new technique becomes habitual and can be performed without conscious thought. With developed tennis strokes this can take over six months, and few people have enough foresight to stay on track this long. Marty did.

His game improved at glacial speed. At the end of the first year, Marty's forehand had become serviceable, and he had made some slight progress at controlling his anger and depression during competition. In his second year, Marty was at least able to practice with the better players on the team and even played six or seven matches against lower-ranked schools. His volley was still nonexistent, his serve only fair, and his head shaky, but he now had a solid set of groundstrokes, and he could face the pressure and frustration of competition without falling apart immediately.

During his third year at Pepperdine, Marty became a solid and valuable member of the team, playing at the sixth singles position and winning almost all of his matches, even against the likes of Stanford, UCLA, and the other top programs that were our rivals. He had developed a sound baseline game and had learned to compensate for his poor nerves and tendency to choke under pressure by simply outlasting opponents mentally and physically. Marty might not perform well on the first big point, or even the second, or the third, but he made up for it by keeping his opponent under pressure and making him work all the time.

It was not a pretty process. Marty would get ahead, have a chance to win, and then get the "winners" chokes and let his opponent back in the match. When he was even or behind, Marty's nerves relaxed, and he would usually play better. Eventually, Marty would get another opportunity to win but might choke again. But this would not discourage him. He would keep struggling, and the games would go back and forth until he got so many opportunities that he would eventually come through on one of them or his opponent would tire of the whole process and give up. This approach proved remarkably effective.

MARTY FINALLY GETS IT

By his fourth year, Marty's volley was getting very good. He had worked diligently on his technique for all these years, and it finally started to pay off. He was a big guy and getting to net became intimidating to opponents. Besides, coming to net was another way to compensate for his tendency to choke on big points. If Marty came to net, his opponent was forced to hit a passing shot, which is a very precise shot and difficult to hit under pressure. His opponent was liable to miss, and Marty would win the point without having to make a shot under pressure himself. (In fact, coming to net is a little like being the dealer in blackjack. The dealer's advantage is that the other player may go over 21 and bust before the dealer even takes a card and has any risk of busting.) Thus armed, Marty moved up to the number two position on the team and was now competitive with most of the top college players.

Since Marty did not play any college matches or tournaments in his first year at Pepperdine, the year did not count against his eligibility allotment. It's called red shirting. Players are allowed a total of four years eligibility, and since Marty had used only three, he was entitled to another year to play on the team. And in this fifth year, Marty really blossomed. He became a fearsome serve and volleyer and swarmed the net at every opportunity. He played number two on the team, was elected team captain, led the team to the NCAA finals, and earned All-American honors in singles. Marty had become one of the best players in intercollegiate tennis. And he continued to improve. He played on the professional tour, reached the final 16 at both Wimbledon and the US Open, was ranked among the top 100 players in the world, and played Davis Cup for Canada—all with limited physical tools but with an uncanny ability to face his fears, understand his problems and work systematically on solving them.

IT WORKS IN BUSINESS TOO

Successful businesspeople apply the same approach with the same results. Leo Wyler, my old boss whom we first discussed in Chapter Seven, claimed that he owed much of his success to his attitude toward problems. Leo said that while most people dread problems, he actually enjoyed solving them. He said he looked at them as "challenges" and "opportunities." And how much easier is it to wrestle with a time-consuming and difficult problem when you are enjoying the processes than it is when you feel put-upon, negative, and in a hurry to be done?

I saw the exact opposite approach lead to the undoing of an acquaintance who had, after twenty seven years, worked his way into the upper middle management of a growing oil services company. This gentleman, let's call him Lew, had worked diligently to reach his position and now, at the age of fifty-five, appeared to have it made. Although Lew's career had leveled off, he was being paid a big salary, had an excellent benefits program and did not have to work too hard. He realized that he was never going to be president of the company but figured that all he had to do for the next few years was to collect his salary, keep out of trouble, push papers around, and eventually retire to the easy life.

Distorting Lew's vista was the fact that he was not terribly bright and had actually reached a corporate position that slightly exceeded his level of competence. Solving complex business problems was not his favorite pastime. Because he felt that no further advancement in the company was possible, Lew lost his drive. He became more interested in his golf and taking long, pleasant lunches than he was in doing a bang-up job and improving the company. He gained weight, slowed down, and went into a holding pattern. In basketball, it would have been equivalent to a team with a lead employing a slow-down, control game in order to run out the clock. He just wanted things to run smoothly and to be left alone. Lew became lazy.

And Lew particularly hated problems. They made him uncomfortable because he wasn't good at solving them. At a deeper level, he was insecure in his ability to do a first rate job in his position, and this made him want to escape his office whenever possible. Problems forced him back to his desk. Moreover, they demanded energy, thought, and, worst of all, work. Lazy and escapist as Lew had become, problems were noxious to his ears. When subordinates came to him with problems that he needed to solve, he would help them if the fix happened to be easy. But if the problem was difficult and the subordinate persisted in asking for a resolution, Lew became resentful. He simply wanted the problem (and the subordinate) to go away. If approached too many times about the same unresolved problem, he became irritated. To avoid his temper, subordinates learned to stay away and live with their problems. But this made them unhappy. They wanted to do a good job, move up in the company, and Lew, as their superior, was an obstacle rather than an asset. He made their jobs harder and less pleasant. Of course, word eventually reached upper management, but they were loath to rock the boat and fire Lew. Besides, business was good, Lew's section was, despite complaints, doing well enough, and they liked him personally.

The situation remained the same for several years. Then, in 1996, the price of oil began a relentless and disastrous (for the oil companies, not the consumers) decline. Oil companies could not afford to drill, and the oil services business was catastrophically impacted. Declining revenues and unhappy stockholders make companies look for ways to cut overhead, and unproductive employees who get large salaries are tempting targets. Needless to say, Lew no longer has his cushy position.

ALEXANDER "THE GREAT" ACTUALLY WENT OUT OF HIS WAY TO FIND PROBLEMS TO OVERCOME

Few individuals in history are as fascinating and have been as utterly success-ful as Alexander "the Great." Having the term "the Great" appended to his name makes even the historically uninformed suspect that this fellow must have been pretty good at something. Let us now attempt to describe what this "something" was.

Alexander's success as a general, organizer, and administrator was without equal in the history of Western Civilization. Starting in 336 B.C. at the age of twenty, he became king of Macedonia (a small, semi-barbaric country located just North of Greece) and proceeded, in the ensuing 13 years, to conquer most of the inhabited world between Greece and India. Starting with a force of 50,000 men, he marched over 19,000 miles, conquering as he went, and, on several occasions, fought battles in which he defeated armies over ten times his army's size. In the course of his campaigns he overthrew the vast Persian Empire, which, for the prior 200 years, had dominated western Asia and, at the time of Alexander's conquest, comprised the largest, wealthiest, and most pow-erful empire yet seen in the western world.

Alone among history's great commanders, Alexander was never defeated, though he fought innumerable battles against formidable foes who employed every imaginable sort of weaponry and tactic in every type of terrain. Stationing himself in the front line of battle, he was able to make unfailingly accurate, split-second tactical decisions under life-threatening duress. Athletic and courageous to an almost mythical degree, he was at personal risk in scores of engagements, wounded in almost every part of his body, yet managed to sur-vive against all odds. Meanwhile, he had the business acumen and people skills to keep his army fed, supplied, reinforced, and motivated while campaigning over mountain barriers and trackless wastes against an endless succession of antagonists. Once conquered, he controlled his vast new territories with his own administrators and oversaw the founding of numerous new cities, the most famous of which was Alexandria in Egypt, which became one of the greatest cities of ancient times and survives even to this day. Never has so much been accomplished by one individual in so little time.

Of course, Alexander possessed all of the traits identified in this book as used by the champions, but foremost among these was his penchant for problem solving. Problems stimulated him. To tell Alexander that a feat had never before been accomplished was to insure that he would undertake it. Its very difficulties attracted him, and Alexander's self-confidence was such that he felt no challenge to be beyond his capabilities. So well-known was this character-istic of Alexander's that there was a Greek word, "pothos," for an "overwhelm-ing urge, when facing formidable obstacles, to attempt the unattainable" which was applied, in ancient times, only to Alexander.

One example of this aspect of Alexander's character was his decision to besiege Tyre, the most powerful trading city in Phoenicia (now Lebanon), situated on a rocky island a half mile offshore, protected by immense walls of up to 150 feet high on its landward side, and considered to be absolutely impregnable. Its rulers offered to remain neutral in Alexander's war with Persia and suggest-ed, evenhandedly, that they would admit neither Macedonians nor Persians to the city.

Alexander had no pressing strategic need to occupy the city. Having recently defeated the Persian ruler, Darius III, at the battle of Issus (in Syria), Alexander needed to consolidate his territorial gains in the eastern Mediterranean area and deal again with Darius III, who had escaped after the battle and was now busy raising a new army of over 500,000 men from his eastern provinces. With no time to waste, Alexander could have easily bypassed and isolated Tyre so that it would have eventually fallen into his hands voluntarily. But Alexander was affronted by its resistance and was determined to bring it to heel regard-less of cost.

He called a halt to his army's progress down the Mediterranean coast toward Egypt, conscripted the local populace into his workforce, and began building a mole (a causeway) to connect the shoreline with the city. This involved a tremendous amount of labor and effort, since the sea averaged over 20 feet in depth and was often lashed with violent winds. Wood had to be cut from trees in distant mountains and hauled to the shore to build a framework, and large rocks were brought up to fill it in. At first, the Tyrians, sitting on their boats just out of missile range, laughed at him and heckled his soldiers as they strained under their burdens. But when the Tyrians saw that the mole was over 200 feet wide and progressing inexorably toward their city, their laughter turned to concern.

The Tyrians brought up ships (they had a more powerful navy than the Macedonians) and began firing arrows and light catapults at the unarmed workers, killing and wounding many. To protect his men, Alexander set up screens of canvas and hides as well as wooden towers from which his archers could shoot down on the attacking enemy ships.

At the same time, Alexander faced other difficulties. The mole had reached deep water, and progress slowed to a crawl. No matter how many rocks the Macedonians tossed into the water, the base of the mole seemed to remain unchanged, far below the surface. In addition, Arab raiders began attacking the soldiers who were cutting wood, choking off much of the timber supply and further slowing the construction process. In the course of these tribulations, the Tyrians made a ferocious attack on the mole itself. They towed a barge filled with incendiaries toward the section that held Alexander's wooden towers and protective screens, and set it afire. When it struck the mole, a huge caldron of naphtha tipped over, ignited, and spread a violent conflagration throughout Alexander's precious towers. At the same time, a flotilla of small Tyrian boats came alongside the mole and poured a barrage of arrows into any Macedonian who dared show his face or fight the fires. Raiding parties landed and set fire to anything not destroyed by the initial blaze. By the time it was over, the attack had left Alexander's towers and equipment a charred mass of rubble and the mole littered, from end to end, with dead bodies.

Undaunted, Alexander rebuilt his towers and screens and continued extending and even widening the mole. But now he realized that he would have to get control of the seas in order to protect his men and ultimately force his attack home. Inside of a month he had collected enough ships from the conquered cities within his domain to overpower the Tyrian navy, bottling up its ships in their harbors and completely blockading Tyre. And to protect his wood supply, Alexander, himself, took a contingent of light-armed troops up into the Lebanese mountains and spent two weeks intimidating the marauding tribesmen.

As the work on the mole continued, Alexander had to contend with the destructive powers of nature itself. A violent storm blew up and threatened the mole. Alexander's engineers managed to position a large number of huge, untrimmed tree trunks in the water beside the mole to blunt the force of the breaking waves. After the storm abated, Alexander's men repaired the damage and even incorporated the tree trunks into the structure of the mole to widen and strengthen it.

Finally, the mole reached the island and Alexander brought up all of his heavy artillery, catapults, rams, as well as huge siege towers with boarding gangways and began a tremendous assault on the walls. The Tyrians were ready and fought back ferociously. Unfortunately for the Macedonians, it was here that the walls were the highest, thickest, and best defended. The Tyrians had built high wooden towers on the wall from which they could rain down a devastating missile attack. In addition, they had constructed a variety of diabolical defensive engines, the nastiest of which was the simplest. They filled heavy cauldrons with sand and gravel, heated the mixture to near incandescence, and tipped the glowing contents out upon any Macedonian soldier within range. The scorching sand got under the soldier's armor and seared its way through flesh to bone. Ultimately, the defenses in this section of the wall proved impregnable, and Alexander was forced to look elsewhere for a weak point.

So he mounted rams and siege towers on ships and began to attack other sections of the wall from the sea. To counter this threat, the Tyrians dumped huge stones into the shallow water at the base of the walls so Alexander's ships could not approach closely enough to use their rams. Alexander responded by anchoring ships with winches underneath the walls, hauling the stones up, and dropping them into the deeper water away from the walls. The Tyrians then sent armored boats among Alexander's ships to cut their anchor cables. Alexander countered by placing similarly armored boats in front of the cables to ward off these attacks. The Tyrians responded with divers who swam underneath the boats to cut the cables (which were made of ropes). Alexander simply replaced the ropes with chains, and, at last, the Tyrians were out of ideas. Alexander kept probing various sections of the wall, ultimately found a vulnerable sector, broke through with his rams, and, after nine months of unrelenting effort, captured the city.

With an ever changing and apparently never ending array of formidable obstacles thrown in his path, what possessed Alexander to continue probing for measures to surmount them? What made him believe that success was ultimately possible? After all, others had tried to take Tyre, yet all had failed. How could he know that there was not some defense so potent that even he could not breach it? The answer is that he didn't have to know, chapter and verse, the exact pathway to success. He had only to believe that all problems have solutions and that if he worked hard enough and long enough, he could discover what they were.

The siege of Tyre was only one of Alexander's many gratuitous flirtations with the impossible. Another was his legendary capture of the "Soghdian Rock," a mountain fortress located in southern Russia just north of present day Afghanistan. As with Tyre, its inhabitants believed it to be utterly impregnable. The Rock itself was a high plateau with sheer faces on all sides, upon which the natives had stationed a large number of troops and where many of the

113

region's inhabitants had come to seek refuge. It was provisioned to withstand a siege of two years, and its summit was covered with deep snow, making an ascent very difficult while providing its inhabitants with an unlimited supply of water.

Alexander called on the people to surrender, offering to allow them to return unmolested to their homes. They responded with derisive laughter, telling him to "find soldiers with wings to capture the Rock for him, as no other sort of person could cause them the least anxiety." Apparently they did not realize that they were angering and challenging the wrong person.

Alexander gathered together an elite force of 300 of his men who had experience at rock climbing and offered a huge reward in talents of gold to the first 12 men who could reach the summit of the backside of the plateau. It would be an extremely difficult and dangerous ascent, but the gold reward would be enough to make the winners rich. The climbers found the steepest and, therefore, the least defended rock-face for their ascent. Starting out at night, they used ropes and iron tent-pegs (pitons) to make good their ascent (during the course of which 30 of them fell to their deaths). The remainder reached the summit by dawn and waived pieces of linen to let Alexander know that they had made it. Alexander sent emissaries to notify the enemies' advanced posts that he had found his "winged soldiers" and that his men were now in possession of the summit of the Rock. The natives turned, saw Alexander's men above and behind them, and panicked. Imagining that there was a large force behind the few they could see, the natives immediately threw down their arms and surrendered.

SUMMARY

Alexander the Great, Leo Wyler, and Marty Laurendeau, each in his own realm, was energized and made optimistic by assuming that there is a solution for any problem. This helped them maintain a high level of drive in the face of setbacks. It led to a positive attitude that, in turn, helped clarify their thinking and opened their minds to novel ideas. Finally and most importantly, they found, as you will, that believing in this assumption usually makes it come true.

SENSITIVITY TO SUCCESS

The champion is extremely sensitive to actions that succeed and fail, quickly adapting subsequent actions to enhance success and avoid failure.

The winners seek information and mentally file away for future use every scrap of available data. More importantly, they see what works. Most learning comes from experience, and the champions are alert. They concentrate intently on the task at hand, learn quickly from their failures and successes, and adjust their behaviors accordingly. Information gleaned from reward and punishment immediately shapes future actions. Champions acquire this sensitivity because they commit themselves so deeply to their tasks. Their high drive sharpens their senses. Wanting so badly to succeed opens their eyes. It focuses their attention and masses their powers of concentration. In this state they are remarkably perceptive. In a word, they work "smart."

Conversely, the less successful are not perceptive and tend to make the same mistakes repeatedly, behaving as if there were no difference between reward and punishment. Because their fears of failure make them shun commitment, they tread only on the surface of life. The task at hand does not fill their viewscreens, and their attentions wander. Their insecurities and self-protective impulses cloud their minds, and they see with half-closed eyes. Not believing deeply in their own capabilities and only too willing to cast their fates to chance, they proceed blindly, making only the shallowest and most perfunctory efforts to understand the competitive scene confronting them. In a word, they work "dumb."

Consider how great tennis players learn where and how hard to hit the ball in particular situations. They learn by trial and error. For example, they may, in one situation, hit the ball to a certain spot and lose the point; later, in the same situation, they may hit the ball to a different spot and win the point. They mentally record the results of these and thousands of other experiences and develop a feeling for which spots are advantageous and which are dangerous. During competition they instinctively use this information to select the shot for each situation that provides the maximum payoff for the minimum risk. People like Andre Agassi and Serena Williams are able to choose with uncanny efficiency the highest percentage reply to any shot their opponents may hit. They never hit the ball one mile per hour harder nor one centimeter closer to the lines than necessary. They develop this judgment by keeping their eyes open and adjusting their strategies in response to what they see. They are sensitive to what works, drawn to it like a shark to blood.

On the other hand, the vast majority of people seem largely oblivious to the lessons of success and failure and respond only to the grossest and most obvious examples. (Champions, by contrast, respond to the slightest nuance.) I saw this in operation at my tennis camps. Each week during the summer, nearly 100 young tennis hopefuls came to my camps at Pepperdine University. For the most part, they were eager to hone their skills and improve their games. My opening talk on strategy focused on the fact that at the lower skill levels of the game, defense has the advantage over offense, and the person that hits the ball in the court the most is usually going to win. Lacking fine accuracy, the person hitting hard, close to the net, and close to the lines takes too many risks and is going to lose. They all nodded in agreement.

Yet, when they got on the court, most of them did what they always had done—hit the ball too hard, too close to the net and lines, and made too many errors. Their take on the situation was that hitting three out of four balls in the court was the best they could do. In reality, though, they needed to hit the ball in the court nine out of ten times, and they could have done so if only they had hit the ball easier and farther away from the net and lines. The few that understood this (and hit easier and more safely) missed less frequently, had a commanding competitive advantage, and won almost all of their matches. Somehow the majority did not respond to the evidence of their senses and continued to overhit, even though they lost again and again to the steadier players. They called the steady players "dinkers," belittled their games, and claimed that the "dinkers" would never get any better playing that way. (They sometimes even felt self-righteous about hitting hard, convinced that the steady players have adopted an inherently immoral style of play.) In the process, they failed to adjust their games in accordance with their capabilities. Rather they continued to hit too hard, miss, and lose.

Why did they do this, despite the evidence of their senses? They did so because the usual bugaboos of insecurity and fear of failure cloud their judgments. It is, simply put, emotionally easier to just bang away at the ball and leave the outcome to fortune than it is to, in a controlled and thoughtful manner, keep the ball in the court. If you have a good day, you win; if you have a bad one, you lose—no emotional drama. By contrast, playing consistently leads to long, stress-filled points. You go nose to nose with your opponent, and the contest becomes an obvious battle of wills. It gets personal, and winning requires emotional discipline and prolonged concentration. Unruly nerves and choking raise their ugly heads and must be overcome. None of this is pleasant, so the average person dodges the situation. They subconsciously realize that if they scrutinize the scene too closely, they might have to take actions that they would rather avoid. So they don't look, and they lose.

THINKING IS HARD WORK

In order to work "smart," the way champions do, you have to be constantly alert. You have to continually take in and process information. In a word, you have to always be thinking about what you are doing, not, as is too often the case, mindlessly plodding through the motions—on mental autopilot. As they plug away on a task or practice a new skill, champions ask themselves questions like, "Is this the easiest way to do it?" "What are my weaknesses, and how can I improve them?" "What is the most important part of the project I am working on?" "Why am I doing it this way instead of that way?" They want to know everything about what they are doing so they can do it better. Their eyes and minds are unceasingly active and vigilant.

In practicing a sport, for example, the champions constantly refine their techniques, and this requires mental effort as well as physical. When working on their groundstrokes, great tennis players focus on getting into perfect position, preparing the shoulder turn early, watching the ball, and any other technical device that has proven helpful to them in hitting the shot better. They concentrate intensely for hours at a time, attempting to rehearse the muscle memory involved in a near perfect stroke. Their goal is to make all motions correct and automatic for use in competition. On the other hand, their less successful contemporaries may put in similar amounts of time on the practice courts and exert similar amounts of physical effort running around and hitting balls, but their minds are often elsewhere, hence their improvement per hour of court time is far less. The less successful are mentally passive during practice, assuming that simply putting in the time and doing the physical work will make them better. Of course they do get better, but not better enough.

Most people habitually avoid mental exertion. Examples are commonplace. Watching television, which is a mentally passive activity, is more attractive to the masses than reading a book, which requires active mental participation. The repellent aspect of exercising is more mental than physical. The mind has to force the body to work, and it is this, rather than the work itself, that most people wish to shun.

Do you need proof? Recall the television ads for those belts that you wrapped around your midsection and which, supposedly, stimulated your abdominal muscles with pulses of electricity and caused them to contract. You saw beautiful young men and women with shapely cut abdominal muscles on these programs, claiming to have gotten their figures by relaxing and watching their favorite television shows while the belts stimulated their muscles. (It seemed too good to be true, and, unfortunately, it was.) But what was the charm of the belts? Your abdominal muscles still had to contract and work in order to become shapely and strong, just as they do with sit ups and crunches. The difference was only in what drove the muscles to work. With the belts, your muscles were driven by external electricity, whereas with normal exercise, the electricity had to be supplied by your brain. And people were willing to pay plenty to escape having to use their brains.

LEARNING QUICKLY FROM SUCCESS AND FAILURE IN BUSINESS

Sensitivity to what works is equally valuable in business. My father-in-law, Bob Novick, has made a substantial fortune in real estate development with a business strategy that I, as a person who relies on detailed analysis and planning, find odd, but strangely effective. He has replaced almost all detailed analysis (which is personally distasteful to him) with sensitivity, flexibility, and relentless energy. He loves making deals and has an excellent sense for putting the right product in the right location. But he likes to fly by the seat of his pants. He depends on alertness, flexibility, and accurate gut instincts. A beehive of activity, Bob never sits still. By constantly moving forward, yet being quick to change direction if he finds that his original course is not working out, Bob somehow gets where he wants to go. It works because he is extremely self-confident, sensitive to the slightest positive or negative nuance, totally flexible, and powered by unlimited bionic energy.

Like Bob Novick, my close friend George Zwerdling also has a knack for seeing what works in business and has been equally successful financially. Having graduated from the Harvard Business School as a Baker Scholar and having spent his early years in business as a consultant for giant corporations, George, unlike Bob Novick, is the consummate analyst. George never makes a move without dissecting every possibility and planning for every contingency. No two people could approach business more differently, yet both have been successful because both are ever on the alert to what is or is not working.

Starting out with nothing but a great brain in the early 1970s, George borrowed enough money to buy a small company that consisted of five small wholesale electronics outlets specializing in the sale of vacuum tubes. George was able to negotiate a bargain price because the owners wanted to retire. Moreover, the company was only marginally profitable, and it looked like it would become even less profitable in the future because it was in a dying business. (Vacuum tubes were, at the time, being replaced by transistors.)

George made a quick analysis of the business. Obviously, he had to somehow cut costs or increase sales or both. George worked out deals with his suppliers to get better prices on his tubes while simultaneously adding electronic items for which the demand was growing rather than shrinking. He was also having difficulty running the stores efficiently. They were widely scattered physically, so it was difficult for him to get to each of them himself, and most were too small to operate efficiently. In these stores the revenues were too small to support strong management, and the weak, inexpensive management that the stores could afford ran them poorly. It was Catch-22.

George sold off four of these stores to raise enough cash to pay off his loans. Then he poured all of his resources into the one good store in Las Vegas where the market was growing rapidly, the managers were excellent, and the competition was weak. He soon saw that the store could serve as an excellent base for a wholesale electronics business, which he started and built up. Ultimately, with no debt, cash in the bank, and a huge, lucrative store and wholesale business in Las Vegas, George became a rich man.

Like the great athletes, George was alert to see what was working and what wasn't and, like them, didn't continue making the same mistakes for long. The essence of his approach was to immediately identify the weak points in his business and to fix them or get rid of them. He rapidly identified the promising area of the business (where it made money) and concentrated his energies there.

WINNERS WANT TO HEAR ABOUT THE PROBLEMS, LOSERS DON'T

Successful people are alert and sensitive to problems. They understand their own weaknesses. They want to find out about them because they want to fix them. The losers, on the other hand, are insecure and don't really believe they can fix the problems, so they would rather not hear about them. They only want to hear the good news. This holds true for business as well as sport.

In their 1988 book, *Lessons of Experience*, authors, McCall, Lombardo, and Morrison describe a group of business executives who started out very successfully but ultimately failed. The researchers determined that these men and women relied almost exclusively on their strengths in doing their work. They made little or no effort to identify their weaknesses and fix them. Ultimately, these weaknesses proved their undoing.

I ran into an example of this kind some years ago when I was consulting for an investment firm. It had acquired a sportswear company (call it Company S). Company S sold its line through its own small chain of retail shops as well as by catalog. It was inefficiently run but still slightly profitable because its products were so clever and attractive that the company was able to charge high prices and extract extraordinarily high markups. The head of the investment company, whom we will call Mr. Smith, liked the products, loved the markups, and was optimistic about expanding Company S. He just needed a good president for Company S to do this for him.

But management at Company S had been an ongoing headache. In the two years since he bought it, Mr. Smith had been forced to replace the president of Company S twice and was spending more time on Company S's affairs than he liked. Mr. Smith did not usually become this involved in his investments, most of which were passive stock positions in public companies. In this case, Mr. Smith was getting in deeper and hearing more than he wanted about Company S's daily affairs, and he was hoping his most recent appointment as president would straighten things out. He wanted to refocus his energies on his own core business.

The new president was a reliable gentleman with an accounting background—excellent with numbers but not experienced in the retail business. Because of this, I suggested that the first order of business should be for him to spend the next few months running a retail store in order to learn the intricacies of retailing from the bottom up. Only then, I felt, could he understand what was behind the numbers on the financial reports and, with any conviction, tell his employees what to do. The new president strongly disagreed and refused to do it. He felt that he could understand the business just fine by talking to the employees and looking at the numbers. Mr. Smith, tired of looking for new company presidents, backed up the president. I was overruled.

The company limped along for the next several years, growing slowly, losing a little money, and was as inefficient as ever. Dissatisfied, Mr. Smith wanted action and faster growth. Eventually he ran across a replacement for the president who was a real hotshot salesman and an aggressive dealmaker. Once in place, this fellow acquired two other companies and bought a huge warehouse to store enormous new inventories. Mr. Smith began to pour millions of dollars into the expansion program, and the losses, explained as necessary in any rapid company expansion, were astronomical.

Rumors from reliable sources began to circulate that the new president was not always truthful and that he might even be involved in certain shady dealings. I brought this to Mr. Smith's attention, and he countered with, "I checked this gentleman out before I hired him, and his character and honesty are impeccable." With that, he cut off further discussion of the matter, and I did not attempt to bring it up again. The prior president, who still worked for Mr. Smith in another capacity, also heard the rumors and attempted to warn Mr. Smith, but he encountered a reception no warmer than mine. "Sour grapes," he was told by Mr. Smith, whose mind was already made up and who simply did not want to hear about such problems. Subliminally Mr. Smith knew that if he acknowledged the problems, he would have to act on them, and he was not prepared to do so.

A year later the bubble burst. It was discovered that the new president was in cahoots with his warehouse manager, and they were both taking kickbacks from suppliers. The warehouse was a mess—hundreds of thousands of dollars of useless inventory were scattered all over the place without proper inventory systems or complete records. The losses totaled in the millions of dollars.

All of this happened because Mr. Smith was not alert to problems, and without this information, he was unable to fix them. He had plenty of early warnings but reacted like a kid who sticks his fingers in his ears and starts singing loudly to drown out unwelcome words from his parents. Mr. Smith ran a wealthy and well-financed investment company that was quite successful investing passively in public stocks. He should have stuck to that business. Mr Smith was not prepared for his role in overseeing an active investment. Yes, his company could afford the losses in this relatively small investment, which would be buried among the profits of his other investments, but there was no need to take such losses. If even one person told him that his president was illicit, he should have investigated or at least become suspicious, and he certainly should have done so after the second warning. The person in charge must be sensitive to what is working and what isn't and take corrective actions early rather than late. He must want to hear problems. Only then can he solve them.

LEO WYLER KEPT HIS EAR TO THE GROUND

By contrast, my old mentor, Leo Wyler, was very successful at running companies because he was studious in gathering information, and one snippet of his always-intelligent advice bears repeating. It came during a dispute between two of his upper management employees. Feelings ran high, and each bad-mouthed the other. One of the disputants was a gentleman of the highest character while the other was not to be trusted. My instinct was to side with the man of excellent character and to discard the defamatory remarks of the other fellow.

Leo was of a different opinion. He said that he always listened carefully to both sides in a dispute in order to gain information about both parties. Although one side might be more right than the other, that is no cause to throw away information. Even the best people are not perfect, and Leo wanted to know what the imperfections were. Even the assertions of the worst people, Leo said, usually have a grain of truth to them. By absorbing all the information, biased and inaccurate as some of it might be, Leo was alerted to areas of potential concern. Upon further investigation, they might turn out to be inconsequential, but Leo wanted to know about them anyway. Leo's theory was, "Forewarned is forearmed." Mr. Smith's theory, by contrast, was, "I don't want to hear about it."

SUMMARY

You must work towards your goals with your eyes wide open. Hard work is helpful but not enough. Lowering one's head and simply grinding forward is apt to be inefficient. You must make a special effort to work with your head up—alert and concentrating so as to soak up and assimilate every bit of available information. At the same time, be wary of a natural urge to discard those facts that are at odds with your preconceived notions, that cause you to change your plans, or that force you to undertake unpleasant tasks. Absorb and employ ALL information so that you work not just hard, but "smart."

REACTION
TO
FAILURE

The champion reacts to failure with increased determination to succeed rather than discouragement.

The successful achiever reacts differently to failure than most people. Losses challenge champions and actually increase their motivation. They become more determined and intense and silently vow to work harder and increase their preparations so that they can win next time. They keep their heads, make necessary adjustments, and become more dogged than ever in their quest for success. As in boxing, the winners must be able to take a punch as well as give one out. There are no champions with "glass jaws."

In contrast, the ordinary person who takes a loss is prone to become discouraged, panicky, less determined, and do something foolish. This is because most people are, to begin with, fearful that they will fail. The loss is proof that their lurking fears were well founded. In their minds, the probability of failure has grown dramatically, and it becomes increasingly difficult for them to hold their heads up and compete with their original vigor. They subconsciously want to escape, so they numb themselves to the pain of failure by damping their desire to win.

TENNIS CHAMPIONS REBOUND
QUICKLY FROM REVERSALS

You can see this in condensed form in a single tennis match. When Jimmy Connors, one of the great competitors of all time, lost a point, he did not get rattled. He simply got tougher on the next point. And if he lost that one, he raised the gain further and tried even harder to win the following point, and so on. With each point that Connors lost, his determination to win the next point grew, and he became increasingly likely to win it. This was a self-stabilizing situation, and it made Connors very difficult to beat. Since he toughened as he got behind, it was very hard for opponents to develop momentum against him. His increasing resistance stopped opponents from winning streaks of points. The losers, by contrast, weaken with each point they lose and become increasingly likely to lose the next point. This is an unstable situation where they are likely to lose streaks of points, spiral into despair, and ultimately fall apart.

When tennis champions lose a match, their instincts are to go to the practice court, work harder, and improve, while those with loser mentalities become disheartened and less inclined to practice. Losses simply motivate the champions to get better. They will assess their weaknesses and strive to fix them. They will get into better physical condition and work to hone their weapons so that the next time they enter the arena they will be better armed. Losses make them increase their activity levels. Their drive to control their fate impels them to take action. They know that if they do nothing the losses will continue, and they are not willing to let that happen. The losers, on the other hand, weaken and do little, if anything, to save themselves from further failures.

You can see that if the champion's approach is applied consistently over time, it will eventually produce a very good tennis player. In like manner, setbacks drive the winner business people to seek, work on, and fix the causes of their setbacks. They are stimulated to additional effort. They think about their problems, turn them over thoroughly in their minds, and develop plans for productive changes. The losers are disheartened and incline toward escape rather than investing more work.

A SETBACK HELPS ME

The biggest tournament I ever won as a junior was the result of a setback. In those days (the mid-1950s), the Los Angeles Tennis Club was the hotbed of tennis in Southern California. The offices of the Southern California Tennis Association were there, and all of the top professionals played at the "Club" when they were in town. Besides the pros there were always other good players around if you wanted a game—and I always did. As one of the top juniors in the area, I was given a guest membership to the Club so that I could practice, improve, and bring glory to the Southern California Tennis Association. I hated losing and was a practice fanatic, so I hung out at the Club all the time.

I theorized that if I practiced more than the other guys, I would eventually beat them.

Unfortunately, I had a somewhat rebellious and anti-establishment nature. I instinctively did not like being told what to do, and this was ultimately bound to lead to a clash with Perry T. Jones, the head of the Southern California Tennis Association and virtual Czar and dictator of tennis in Southern California. One afternoon I was practicing on one of the back courts at the Club when Mr. Jones walked up and told me to vacate the court because the members might want to use it. As I walked off, I noticed that there were at least a half dozen empty courts, so I asked Mr. Jones why I had to stop practicing since there seemed to be plenty of spare courts. And, I added, I had a guest membership to the Club, so I was authorized to practice when I wanted anyway. Although I said it as nicely as I could, Mr. Jones took this as an affront to his authority and stormed off muttering, "We'll see about your guest membership." Later that day, I was informed that my guest membership had been revoked. I was then relegated to the public courts and mediocre practice opponents.

But the Southern California Junior Championship was scheduled for the following month, and I set about preparing with a vengeance. I figured that Mr. Jones had his hopes pinned on Bob Delgado, the number one seed and highest ranking player from the previous year, and I intended to beat Bob, win the tournament, and force Mr. Jones to deal with me. Although I was always a hard worker, now I doubled my efforts. I did extra roadwork to improve my conditioning and virtually camped out on the practice courts. If there was no one to play with, I practiced my serve or hit balls on the backboard. I intended to win the tournament if it killed me. When competition began, my concentration was ferocious. I had something to prove, which was my usual reaction to a challenge.

I ended up winning the tournament, beating Bob Delgado in the finals, and, as the top junior in Southern California, was reinstated into Mr. Jones' good graces. My expenses were paid to represent Southern California in the National Junior Championships at Kalamazoo, Michigan, and my guest privileges at the Los Angeles Tennis Club were reinstated.

There are two lessons in this. One is, of course, that reacting productively to a setback is key to success. But the other is that I would have been wiser to have kept my mouth shut in the first place. (This little anecdote would fit well in

Chapter Seven on not taking actions that lead one away from one's goals.) Questioning Mr. Jones was a bad idea. It was motivated by my inherent anti-authoritarianism rather than by my logic system. My logic system would have been concerned with protecting my own best interests and would have concluded that these were not well-served by risking a fight with Mr. Jones over an afternoon's practice. Fortunately I got smarter as I got older.

COUSIN FRED REBOUNDS FROM BUSINESS DISASTER

My cousin, Fred Kayne, showed me a fine example of how a winner businessman handles a serious setback. But let's start at the beginning. Fred always wanted to be rich. Even as a kid, he was constantly involved in starting up little businesses and invariably managed to make a few dollars. In fact, the first money I ever earned was at 13 years of age as Fred's partner in a summer lawnmowing business. Later Fred graduated from MIT in engineering (he obviously was not stupid) and, in the late 1960s, entered the investment business as a stockbroker. He spent the next several years developing a client base and a firm grasp of the intricacies of the business, and, by 1970, Fred was well-respected in the Los Angeles financial community and ready to move up.

His chance came when the small Eastern brokerage firm of Newburger, Loeb & Co. decided to open up offices in Los Angeles. They concluded that Fred would be an ideal guy to build up the new office because his powerful personality would enable him to recruit, control, and motivate a cadre of high producing stockbrokers. They were not wrong. By coincidence, I had also joined Newburger, Loeb, but my job was in the investment banking department. I did not, at first, work directly with Fred, but I did get to see him in action at relatively close range. (In case the readers think I am lauding Fred simply because he is my cousin—forget it. Fred and I both have strong personalities, and our relationship has not always been totally congenial. As kids, we spent summers together and, too often, ended up fighting it out on the lawn. But despite our occasional clashes, I do have immense respect for Fred's talents, morality, and personal qualities.)

And Fred did a great job at Newburger, Loeb. He brought big brokers and wealthy customers into the firm and was responsible, directly and indirectly, for much of the profit of the West Coast office. This profit, in turn, was so large as to provide a substantial portion of the firm's total profit. Fred was made a partner.

He soon learned, however, that the firm was in financial difficulty due to a number of poor management decisions. Fred correctly concluded that he had become a backseat passenger on a ship that was heading for the falls. He felt that the ship could be saved, but not by the crew that had gotten it into trouble in the first place. Fred decided that he would either have to leave or take over management of the firm himself. (Fred has never been short of self-confidence.) Fortunately, the other partners agreed with him, made Fred managing partner, and, in a financial restructuring, Fred became a major shareholder of the new corporate entity, Newburger, Loeb & Co., Inc. Under his direction it prospered, and, a year later, it was sold to a larger investment-banking firm, making Fred a multi-millionaire (for the first time). This was a much bigger deal then than it is now. In those days, you could buy a house in Beverly Hills for $200,000, while that same house now would cost three or four million dollars. Fred was, in my opinion (but not his), comfortably rich.

In any case, Fred was not content to sit back and count his money. He continued running the West Coast office for the new owners, became involved in the investment banking end of the business, and personally invested heavily in the stock market. Then the oil crisis hit in 1973. Cars were stalled in lines at the gas pumps; the economy went into a tailspin; the stock market plummeted; and the stock brokerage business imploded. In the process, Fred, whose largest investment was in a company that manufactured recreational vehicles, lost all of his money and was left with several hundred thousand dollars of debt and no immediate prospects for repaying it.

Many people in this situation would have declared bankruptcy. Fred never considered it. Still, more people would have been horribly discouraged, and a few might have looked for open windows in the nearest high-rise. Fred went back to work. Reflecting years later on his situation, he said two things, in particular, helped him. One was that he didn't look backward and bemoan his fate. He never mentally whined about how unfortunate he had been to make particular investment decisions. Rather, he made note of his mistakes and vowed not to make the same ones again. (He says he makes different ones now.) Then he coldly assessed his situation, took stock of his skills and assets, set short-term realistic goals, and got moving.

A second helpful agendum, Fred noted, was that he never allowed himself to talk about his problems in public or to appear discouraged. Fred was careful to maintain a confident, forceful, and positive outward manner. He correctly reasoned that discouragement and depression make a person appear weak and

129

that in business, people who appear weak are shunned. Fred needed all the influence and power he could muster to rebuild his position.

He took a job with Bear, Stearns & Co., another smallish ($30 million in capital at the time) New York based investment banking firm, running their Century City office. The mid-1970s were hard times for the investment business. During that period approximately 150 investment companies closed their doors. Nonetheless, Fred built the Century City office into the largest and most profitable office of Bear Stearns, and in 1977 he was offered a partnership. He took it, even though it entailed a salary cut that forced him to dip into his savings to meet living expenses. It proved to be the best move he ever made.

By 1979 Bear Stearns' annual profits had jumped to about $100 million and stayed there until the firm went public in 1985. The value of Fred's equity position, which was now in public stock, leapt to over $25 million (according to public record) and he never looked back, amassing an imposing fortune since that time by owning and building up a variety of small companies. Fred just says he was very lucky to be in the right place at the right time.

In my opinion, luck had very little to do with it. Fred's resilience in the face of disaster, his practicality, his driving work ethic, and his recognition that he was particularly skillful in identifying, attracting and motivating talented people combined to position him well. People who do things like this virtually always "get lucky." It's like poker. Good poker players know the odds, read their opponents shrewdly, and make the right moves. They well-nigh invariably win in the long run because the odds are in their favor, not because they are lucky. By contrast, there is not enough luck in the world to turn bad poker players into consistent winners.

COURAGE IN THE FACE OF DISASTER SUSTAINS ROME

The rise of Rome provides an illustration of how this trait works on a national scale. Rome's ascent to world domination is analogous to the rise of a successful athlete or business person. All three must bear numerous defeats and disappointments bravely, learn lessons from them, adapt, and then continue to struggle toward their goals. (The following may appear a bit detailed for readers who are not historically minded, but the detail is necessary to get a realistic feel for the magnitude of the setbacks that the Romans suffered.)

Rome began as a simple military outpost on a crossing of the Tiber River. By the time it became a republic in 508 B.C., it still only controlled an area of 350 square miles. Surrounded by powerful enemies, even its continued existence was in doubt. Yet, step-by-step, Rome rose to become the dominant power in the Western world, eventually turning the entire Mediterranean Sea into a "Roman Lake."

One of the most important secrets of Roman success was in how they reacted to defeat. Their strength was in their unshakable resolve. Rome suffered many military catastrophes, some of such magnitude that few other nations could have survived, yet these setbacks served only to make the Romans more determined. They were never turned from their purposes. Instead of conceding defeat or negotiating settlements, they rebuilt their armies, redoubled their efforts, and continued to fight until fortune finally turned in their favor. In addition to their substantial political and organizational skills, the Romans were incredibly resilient and persistent.

ROME'S INITIAL EXPANSION IS FRAUGHT WITH FAILURES

In her early years Rome gradually overpowered her neighbors one after the other—in the North, the Sabines and Etruscans; in the South, the Latins and Volscians, as well as a host of others—until, by early in the third century B.C., they had become the masters of most of Italy. But their ascent was interrupted by terrible reverses. In 390 B.C. the Romans were routed by the Gauls at the river Allia, and Rome itself was occupied and sacked. Their city was so devastated that some citizens wanted to abandon the site and move to a new capital. Their leader, Camillus, talked them into remaining, and the government helped the people rebuild. But in their weakened state, they were attacked repeatedly by their previously defeated neighbors, the Volscians, Latins, Aequi, and Hernici, and it took fifty more years of intermittent fighting before these peoples could again be brought under the Roman yoke. In the meantime, the Gauls, who had, by now, permanently settled in the far North of Italy, attacked Rome in 367 B.C., 358 B.C., and 350 B.C. and were, each time, repulsed. Afterward, Rome engaged in three savage conflicts against the Samnites for control of Southern Italy and, in 321 B.C., suffered one its worst defeats at Claudine Forks. The beaten Roman army was forced to "pass under the yoke" (an arch of enemy spears) to confirm their submission, and the consuls (the leaders at the front) signed a degrading peace treaty. Back in Rome the Senate repudiated the treaty, and the war continued, though now the Samnites were

131

joined by the Etruscans and Gauls. Thirty more years of fighting were required before the Romans were victorious.

KING PYRRHUS DEALS ROME SEVERAL BLOWS

Next, Rome moved to bring the Greek cities in Southern Italy under her suzerainty. Most of them yielded peacefully but Tarentum resisted, calling on Pyrrhus, King of Epirus (a Greek city-state), for help. Pyrrhus, who was regarded as one of the great warrior-kings of his time and always eager for a fight, arrived with his army and defeated the Romans at Heraclea (280 B.C.) in a battle so bloody that the victors emerged only slightly less shattered than the vanquished. But now all the Greek cities in Italy joined Pyrrhus along with the Samnites and several other former Roman allies. With this strong negotiating position, Pyrrhus sent envoys to Rome seeking peace, along with 2,000 Roman prisoners who were freed on their promise to return if peace were refused. The Roman senate, at the urging of blind old senator, Appius Claudius, refused to make peace so long as foreign troops remained on Italian soil and returned the 2,000 Roman soldiers to Pyrrhus. The war continued and Pyrrhus won another victory in which he again lost almost as many men as the Romans. Still, the Romans showed no signs of weakening. They were prepared for yet another battle, but Pyrrhus had had enough. He packed up his remaining troops and left. (From this incident was coined the phrase "Pyrrhic victory," which is a victory so costly that the victor pays a higher price than the victory is worth.)

HANNIBAL BRINGS ROME TO ITS KNEES

Rome's most severe test came at the hands of Hannibal, the ingenious Carthaginian general, who, in 218 B.C., led his men over the Alps into Italy, much as Napoleon did 2,000 years later. Allying himself with contingents of Spaniards, Gauls, and Africans, Hannibal first defeated the Romans, led by one of the famous Scipios, in a cavalry engagement at the river Ticino.

Stung and aggressive, the Romans, with a full army of 40,000 infantry and 4,000 cavalry, attempted to retaliate against Hannibal's 20,000 infantry and 10,000 cavalry at the river Trebia. The Romans were practitioners of the brute force method of military strategy, relying on hitting the enemy head on, fighting man to man with short swords, and winning with courage and discipline. Hannibal, on the other hand, was a master strategist. He relied on cavalry charges, elephants, ambushes, flank attacks, and a multitude of other surprises to defeat enemy forces numerically superior to his own. At the Trebia he bamboozled and encircled the Romans, killing 25,000 of them, and so impressed the Gauls of Northern Italy that virtually all of them defected to the Carthaginian cause. The Romans were getting into trouble.

In order to put an end to Hannibal once and for all, the Romans raised another army under the command of Gaius Flaminius. Always aware of the personal weaknesses of his opponents, Hannibal taunted the new army's impetuous leader until, blundering after Hannibal, Flaminius was ambushed in a defile between a hillside and the shore of Lake Trasimene. Here, as the Romans marched in the morning mist, Hannibal suddenly launched his hidden troops down the hillside into the unprotected Roman flank. The Romans were trapped against the lake, butchered, and their entire army was lost.

News of this unmitigated disaster struck like a dagger to the heart of the Roman people, but only three days later, more awful news arrived of the destruction of 4,000 Roman cavalry under Gaius Centenius. Rome was now unprotected, and even the stalwart Roman Senate was shaken by this unbroken series of debacles. Polybius, the Greek historian who wrote in the second century B.C., said of this situation, "It is when the Romans stand in real danger that they are most to be feared…" and the Romans remained steadfast. No word of peace was uttered, and the Romans prepared to continue the stubborn defense of their lands. They raised yet another army, even larger in size, and took the field again.

Time passed without a conclusive battle until leadership of the army fell under the joint commands of Gaius Varro, a headstrong, demagogic plebian, and Aemilius Paulus, a respected aristocrat. These two consuls, who commanded the army on alternate days, differed in their inclinations, Paulus wisely advising caution and Varro looking for an immediate showdown. Hannibal, always alert to the psychology of his opponents, concentrated on insulting Varro to raise his already elevated temperature. Unfortunately for Rome, Varro finally got his way on a plain near the town of Cannae, the resulting engagement becoming the most famous battle of annihilation in the history of warfare.

Eighty thousand Roman legionaries, the finest and most disciplined troops in the ancient world, faced Hannibal's 40,000 infantrymen. Although the Carthaginians had a larger force of cavalry, the genius of Hannibal himself was their only real advantage. And that genius devised a battle plan that destroyed almost the entire Roman army, leaving more than 50,000 legionaries dead on the field (equivalent to all the losses suffered by the United States in all the years of war in Viet Nam). How, one may ask, could so few kill so many with-

133

out some advantage in weaponry? The answer is that a man is dangerous if he is attacked from the front, but helpless if attacked from the side or the back. Hannibal managed to encircle the Romans, squeeze them together into a formless, helpless mass, and butcher them.

The news hit Rome like a clap of thunder, and the people were paralyzed with fear, expecting Hannibal and his hordes to appear at the city gates momentarily. Three days later they learned that general Lucius Postumius was ambushed by Celts and his entire army wiped out, making it seem, as Polybius puts it, "as though Fortune herself had taken sides against them in their struggle, and had filled their cup of tribulation to overflowing." Polybius goes on to describe how the Roman reaction to these disasters ultimately led to victory. "In spite of these blows the Senate left nothing undone that was in its power to do. It encouraged the people, strengthened the defenses of the city, and considered the facts of the situation in a brave and manly spirit and the events that were to follow bore witness to its steadfastness. For although the Romans had beyond any dispute been worsted in battle and their military reputation annihilated, yet through the peculiar virtues of their constitution and their ability to keep their heads they not only won back their supremacy in Italy and later defeated the Carthaginians, but within a few years had made themselves masters of the whole world."

SUMMARY

Boxing matches are not necessarily won by the fighter with the most powerful punch. The ability to take a punch and absorb punishment without collapsing, flinching, whining, losing one's head, or becoming disheartened is equally important. Victory usually goes to the courageous, the resilient, and the persistent.

CAPACITY FOR WORK

The champions have an extraordinary capacity for work and understand the direct connection between amount of effort and success.

Thomas Edison said it best when he claimed that success was 1 percent inspiration and 99 percent perspiration. The student of Edison's life can only marvel at the great man's tireless tenacity. Intolerant of laziness, Edison slept little (often working 20 hour days) and accomplished much. He is the most prolific patent holder in American history (1,093 patents), among which were the electric light bulb, the motion picture projector, talking motion pictures, the phonograph, the stock ticker tape, the electric voting machine (where was this machine in the presidential election of 2000?), as well as improvements in the telephone and telegraph. While he was at it, he founded the Edison Electric Light Company to generate and deliver electric power to homes in New York so they could run his electric lights. This later evolved into the General Electric Company.

Edison was a great believer in the method of trial and error for solving certain problems. This depends upon having sufficient energy to slog through a myriad of failures until you stumble on a success. It also depends, of course, on not becoming weakened or debilitated by fears of failure. Edison looked at failure as a necessary stepping stone on the way to success. He demonstrated his mind-boggling persistence by trying over 6,000 different filament materials for his electric light bulb before ultimately happening upon a workable one. Never discouraged by failure, Edison carried out 10,000 unsuccessful experiments trying to develop his storage battery and was reputed to have responded to detractors, "Why I've not yet failed. I've just found 10,000 ways that won't work."

In general, the winners in all areas have a far greater capacity for work than the average person. They put forth extraordinary efforts in their dogged pursuits of chosen goals. Fears of failure are thrust aside and, with no guarantees of success, they are willing to risk total commitment to mastering their tasks. At work, they arrive early and leave late. On the athletic fields they put in extra hours practicing their skills. And their efforts are not just physical. They also concentrate harder than other people so that they work "smart." The champion's unspoken but binding assumption is: "If I work harder and longer than other people, I will eventually win." This is an almost childishly simple strategy, and many of us ignore it because we have had it preached to us, in one form or another, since we were kids. Nonetheless, it offers one of the most powerful, effective, and surest available pathways to success.

Newsweek magazine interviewed five of the all-time greatest athletes in their sports (Wayne Gretzky, Michael Jordan, Martina Navratilova, Joe Montana, and Tiger Woods) and asked them to identify the most important factors leading to their success. Guess what they agreed upon as the number one factor. Of course, old-fashioned hard work. They emphasized that repetition ingrains habits, and habits functioning properly under pressure are what produce victory. They were never satisfied, even when they dominated their sports, and continued to practice and work fanatically throughout their careers. To this day, Tiger Woods is legendary, during tournaments, for hitting endless numbers of golf balls, even into the fading light of evening, in attempting to further perfect his techniques.

The unsuccessful, on the other hand, are unwilling to pull out all the stops and make maximal sustained efforts to achieve their goals. Why? First, for the obvious reason that working long, hard hours is not always as pleasant as playing video games and drinking milkshakes. A more subtle reason follows from the axiom stated earlier: The harder one tries, the greater the pain one suffers if one fails. Insecurities and subconscious fears of failure make most people unwilling to devote extraordinary efforts to any task in which success is not guaranteed. They instinctively shrink back from investing their fullest measure of effort, commitment, and emotion to any project. Were they to do so and fail, they fear that it will show they simply lack whatever it takes to win. They are afraid to find that the totality of their efforts may still bring them up short. So they just don't work hard enough.

THE WORKERS WIN IN TENNIS

As a tennis coach, for example, I considered "work capacity," the ability to put in extraordinary hours of concentrated effort for extended periods of time, to be a talent, equivalent to, or even superior to, physical talent. It reminds me of the joke about the young man from out of town who had tickets for a concert at Carnegie Hall but could not find the famed auditorium. Late and desperate, he approached a well-dressed New Yorker and asked, "Say, how do I get to Carnegie Hall?" The answer, "Practice, son, practice."

Marty Laurendeau understood the correlation between work and performance, and this was a crucial factor in his ultimate ascendancy over the hordes of people more physically gifted than he was. Conversely, people who lack this understanding rarely achieve much, regardless of talent. Picture two tennis players of equivalent skill level. All else being equal, if one of them practices four hours a day and the other only two, who do you imagine will be better in a year? In two years? In five years? The gap will, of course, widen with time. In a month there may be little difference, but over the long term, the player who puts in substantially more time is going to be superior with almost 100 percent certainty.

Obvious as this concept might appear, surprisingly few people truly understand it, and even fewer apply it. Physical talent is a far more common commodity. During my last year coaching, I had on my team one of the most physically gifted athletes I had ever worked with. He was a Swede who had been ranked third in his country in the juniors and who could do virtually anything on the tennis court. He was fast, strong, had wonderful touch; possessed an uncanny sense of where to hit the ball and how hard to hit it; anticipated where his opponent was going to hit the ball; and had excellent nerves and competitive skills. It was hard to think of anything this beautiful athlete lacked. He should have become a high-ranking tennis professional.

But he had one failing, and it was fatal. He believed that two hours of practice a day was sufficient. In fact, he was convinced that more than this actually hurt his game and that he lost feel for the ball and became stale. And nothing I said had the slightest impact on him. I could not pry him away from this belief. Consequently, he became good, but not great. He was an All-American collegiate player but not a professional, and he had the physical and mental ability, if accompanied by sufficient practice, to have become one of the world's best.

137

Of course, a genius might have become a world champion with only two hours of daily practice, but this young man was not such a genius. He needed four hours.

THE WORKERS SUCCEED IN SPORTS AND SCHOOL

A number of studies have confirmed the relationship between amount of work and achievement, both in sport and academia. In areas as diverse as chess, music, and Olympic athletics, researchers have found that a common factor in reaching the highest levels of achievement is the individual's capacity to maintain an arduous regimen of training. For example, in comparing the 1992 Chinese and American Olympic diving teams, researchers noted that the twelve-year-old Chinese performers had already put in as many lifetime practice dives as their American counterparts who were in their early twenties. A 1988 study by K. Anders Ericsson of Florida State University and German colleagues showed that the top echelon violinists in Berlin's finest music academy had put in an average of ten thousand practice hours by their early twenties while the second echelon students had averaged only seventy-five hundred hours. And the astounding success of Asian-Americans in our country's most prestigious academic institutions and professions correlates more closely with their work ethic than it does with their IQ level. Asian-Americans tested only two or three points higher in IQ than Caucasians, but Stanford sociologist Sanford Dorenbusch found that they put in 40 percent more time doing homework in high school than did their schoolmates. She noted, "While most American parents are willing to accept a child's weak areas and emphasize the strengths, for Asians, the attitude is that if you're not doing well, the answer is to study later at night, and if you still don't do well, to get up and study earlier in the morning. They believe that anyone can do well in school with the right effort."

CHAMPIONS WORK HARDER WHEN THEY LOSE

When tennis champions lose a match, their responses are usually to work harder and practice more, partially in order to improve skills and partly out of penitence for the failure for which they accept blame. The tennis teams I coached at Pepperdine were generally ranked among the top five teams nationally and consisted of players that had distinguished themselves individually with high national rankings in junior competition before coming to Pepperdine. These guys hated to lose. One year we traveled in the early season to Miami where we lost to Clemson and SMU, both ranked below us, and barely squeaked out a victory over Miami, also ranked below us. It was a devastating, confidence-shaking opening to our season, and everyone felt that something needed to be done to turn the situation around.

I am not the kind of coach that is so win-crazed that I get emotional after losses and berate or punish teams that have tried their hardest but simply performed below par. These things happen. But this team was highly motivated, and they knew they should have performed better. They expected, even subconsciously WANTED, me to punish them. They wanted me to take action of some kind. They did not want to just roll over and accept the losses as if a normal event had occurred. They wanted to work to control the situation, to do something. They didn't say this, but I could sense it.

So I gave them a stern lecture on how they were going to work their butts off thereafter in practice, and, to show them I meant business, I took them directly to the track and made them run three hard miles. They reached the track exhausted, having each played a singles and a doubles match under a hot Miami sun, so the run was particularly grueling. Afterwards, however, they felt better for it, and on the plane trip home, their spirits actually became positive. This team went on to reach the NCAA finals and achieve the number two ranking in the nation.

MOST PEOPLE BELIEVE THEY WORK HARD

Most people pay lip service to the virtues of hard work. On a verbal basis they recognize that it leads to success. In fact, they actually believe they do work hard, and maybe for them, they do. But relative to champions, their efforts are miniscule. They think they are working hard enough because most of the people around them work no harder than they do. They don't realize that the people they are using for yardsticks are mediocre achievers for the same reasons they are—because they don't work hard enough to excel.

The champions, in contrast, understand the competitive nature of hard work. They understand that "hard work" in itself is not enough. Their concepts are that they must work harder than their rivals. This was brought home to me at the Thunderbird tennis tournament in Phoenix when I was in my early twenties. Having reached the finals with a tough semifinal win earlier in the day, I was, as usual, back on the courts in the late afternoon trying to work a few kinks out of my game. As I practiced, my opponent for the next day's final, Tut Bartzen, wandered by, dressed smartly in slacks and sport shirt and obviously ready to call it a day. At the time, Tut was in his early thirties and had been ranked among the top five men in the United States for most of the past decade. (He won the US National Clay Court championship on five occasions during that time.) A taciturn Texan, Tut stopped, watched silently for a few minutes, and then muttered to me, "Fox, you're psyching me out!" He turned around, changed back into his tennis clothes and spent an hour working on his game too. Tut just couldn't stand the thought of my getting an edge on him. I mention Tut's age because it is easier to work long, hard hours on the tennis court when you are young than when you are over 30. (At 25 your body wants to run. At 35 it will still run, but you have to force it to do so.)

The great tennis players don't just practice more than their opponents, they practice much more. For example, Pancho Gonzalez (one of the greatest players of all time) was even more fanatic than Tut. In 1966, at the age of 38, Pancho was still one of the best in the world, yet he did not stint on the length of his practice sessions. During this time I would sometimes meet Pancho at the LA Tennis Club for afternoon practice sessions. He would have already had a morning session but insisted that we play three out of five set practice matches, which often lasted over three hours. This meant that he was putting in over five hours of work a day, which, on concrete courts, is awfully tough on an older body. But he hated losing and figured that staying in great shape was the best way to avoid doing too much of it.

It is surprising how little work most people are willing to put in, even when their goal is to become a professional athlete, and they should know better. Hank Greenberg, one of the greatest pure hitters in the history of baseball, in his life's story talked about coming to the ballpark early when he was in the minors and paying people to shag balls for him while he practiced hitting. Doing extra work seemed sensible to Hank since he was not a gifted athlete and wanted to make a career out of professional baseball. How else, reasoned Hank, could he improve enough to make the majors? Yet on all those mornings at the ballpark, he was the only player on the team out there practicing. Hank was puzzled. Why wouldn't the other players, who also had hopes of making the majors, come out early to get in extra practice? What could be more important for advancing their careers? Hank could never fathom the answer because he had the mind of a champion and the others didn't.

THE HARD WORKERS WILL SUCCEED IN ANY FIELD

I was reading an article recently by a very successful businessman in which he made the point that putting in longer hours at one's desk, staying late or skipping lunch, may be counterproductive. He felt that working "smart" was better than working "long" and that many people just grind away unproductively. Their work ethic leads them to believe that simply abusing themselves with long hours has some benefit, in and of itself.

I am sure this view has merit in some cases, but its message is misleading. Just choosing to work longer hours does not mean that one will work stupidly. Working long and smart is, of course, the best of all. For example, successful scientists and successful musicians become deeply engrossed in their work and put in incredible numbers of hours—of smart work. Entrepreneurs running successful businesses do the same. And dedicated, disciplined employees in the corporate world are the ones who tend to come in early and stay late—and move up.

SUMMARY

You cannot control your level of talent, but you can control the amount of work you invest in reaching your goals. Working harder and longer will give you a tremendous competitive advantage. Because most people are unwilling to do this, your willingness to exert extraordinary effort can be your surest means to success.

WORK
WITHOUT
IMMEDIATE REWARD

*The champion can continue to work and remain
highly motivated for long periods of time
in the absence of reward.*

For the champions, success does not have to be immediate. They have the acuity to see past the plateau to the peak beyond, and even when no return is visible on the near horizon, they can keep working with high intensity. Champions are not dependent on immediate reinforcement to drive their efforts. By contrast, most people need tangible success relatively quickly, lest they lose motivation, become disheartened, and stop working. (Of course, this concept is related to the previous chapter on work capacity, but its import makes it worthy of special focus. It is one of the factors that contributes to the champions' extraordinary work capacity, but is, by no means, identical with it.)

This ability to delay reinforcement is vital in tennis because stroke technique is critical to success. Tennis strokes must be perfected by years of painstakingly repetitive practice so that the ball can be hit both hard and accurately. Progress is slow, and most people, though they can work hard for a week or two, quickly tire of this process. They cannot keep going without being continuously massaged psychologically with immediate, discernible results. Yet a champion can work for months on a stroke without seeing any improvement or, more distressing still, actually watch the stroke deteriorate for a while before getting better. This drives the weak-minded off. Champions routinely set reasonable goals and then work day after day on them without seeming to improve. They have the unusual ability to remain motivated while delaying gratification.

Stanford psychologist Walter Mischel did a delayed-gratification study on four year-old children. They were given a choice. They could have one marshmallow immediately, or, if they were willing to wait 20 minutes, they could have two. Obviously, the children choosing to wait 20 minutes for the extra marshmallow were the ones who could delay gratification in order to attain a goal. It was unpleasant for them to sit for 20 minutes looking at the marshmallows on the table and not be able to eat one. Some even hid their eyes so they wouldn't have to look at these alluring treats while they waited. They were able to force themselves to do what they thought was right in the face of some discomfort. Even at this early age, this group could overpower their emotional impulses (to stuff marshmallows into their mouths immediately) with their intellects that told them they would benefit by waiting.

Twelve to fourteen years later these same children, now adolescents, were tracked down, and the differences between the groups that could delay gratification and those that couldn't were noted. The most dramatic result was that the ones who delayed gratification scored 210 points higher on their SAT tests than the ones who didn't. They were the better students as well as being substantially more socially adept. In fact, their response to the marshmallow test was a better predictor of SAT performance than even IQ. Socially, they were described as self-reliant, self-assertive, confident, trustworthy, dependable, able to cope well with frustration and stress, and tending to handle challenges by pursuing them rather than giving up in the face of difficulties—all traits that will stand them in good stead at achieving life's goals.

The group who needed immediate gratification were seen as less well socially adjusted, being more stubborn, mistrustful, indecisive, prone to jealousy, resentful that they were not getting their due, over-reactive to irritations and argumentative. Because success in so many areas depends on social skills, these are all traits that will prove a hindrance to this group's achievement potential.

BUSINESS SUCCESS IS RARELY QUICK

It is very unusual for anyone, no matter how talented or intelligent, to make a great deal of money in business right away. Education is helpful; intelligent advice is useful; but nothing can replace experience—and amassing sufficient experience takes time. Dues must be paid by spending time-in-grade and investing in sweat equity, with little financial reward to show for it. Economic advancement rarely comes as soon as the young business person expects, for a number of subtle reasons, and the successful must be able to stay sharp and motivated for a long time without seeing a lot of money.

Most bright, ambitious people entering a business are able to learn 95 percent of the necessary and available information in the first year or two. After that, the work becomes largely routine and repetitious, the pay level doesn't seem to be in any hurry to rise, and most aspirants begin to wonder if they are just wasting time and going nowhere. What they don't realize is that the missing five percent of the necessary information is where all the significant money is made. And this five percent takes another five to ten years to gather and assimilate. It is where all the nuances lie and is the part that people who are not successful never truly understand. The unsuccessful lose their patience, ambition, and hope before they get it. They quit, change professions, or simply plod along. They are defeated because they need immediate reward, and without it, their youthful, alert optimistic attitude—the attitude of winners—dissipates too quickly. They cannot see the peak on the other side of the valley.

The people who remain sharp and hungry over the years will absorb the last five percent. They will ultimately understand, at a gut level, such subtleties as how to close a sale; what level of trust one can ascribe to co-workers, employees, suppliers, and customers; how to handle people and get them to do what one wants; where the real danger points in the business lie; etc. This information only comes with personal experience, and it takes many more years to garner than the neophytes expect. Within this crucial last five percent they will soak up all the essential pieces of the business, their relative importance, and the broad perspective of how it all works together. It is this level of deep experience and knowledge that allow them to not only play the game, but more importantly, to win the game. Only then can one advance and make substantial money.

The analogy in sport might be that beginning tennis players, with sufficient effort, can learn to hit forehands and backhands well in a couple of years. They look good, but lose. It takes five to ten years before players learn the subtleties of the game—the strategies, how to pick on an opponent's weakness, what an opponent is likely to do in certain situations, how to deal with nerves, how to close out sets and matches, etc.—and only then do they really know how to win. Only then can they become champions.

TOP TENNIS PLAYERS NEED TO FORGO IMMEDIATE REWARDS

I always advised young players of the top college level to get out of tennis when their playing days were over. This went against their normal inclination, which was to stay in the game. Tennis was the arena that they knew best and where they could make the most money the quickest. They could immediately start teaching tennis at a club and make $40 to $50 per hour or more. That was very tempting when they compared it to starting at the bottom in some other mundane line of work, where they were totally inexperienced, made less money, and were nobodies. Yet taking the quick money and going for immediate reward would be the sucker play. Their incomes would top out quickly. On the other hand, if they were willing to forego immediate reward and spend the necessary years doing dog work on the cheap to learn a business, they would realize a rich pay-off in the end.

As a tennis coach, I was involved in more than just the athletic careers of my players. I spent many years with these young men in a variety of circumstances where I was the surrogate parent, since their own parents were often far away. I admired most of them as people, and, as most coaches do, I could not help but became personally interested in their futures.

My advice to them was usually the same, "Play tennis for fun, but remember that it's only a game. Go as far as you can in tennis without giving up your other options. Get a good education and realize that making a good living playing professional tennis tournaments is a long-shot. When you've had enough, get out of tennis and go into business—any business. Stick with it, and you will make more money than you dreamed possible."

The top tennis players (like most great athletes) are unusual people. They possess most of the characteristics of champions that I describe in this book—that is why they became top tennis players in the first place. But they don't realize it. Most of their experience is with their fellow top players, who have the same winning personality characteristics as they do. They do not realize that most of the people in the world are not like them and that when they compete against ordinary people, they are like sharks in a school of shrimp. For example, the players I am referring to are among the top 1,000 tennis players in the world. (Imagine how wealthy they would be if they were among the top 1,000 business people in the world.) To reach this level, they have surpassed millions of others who have tried and failed. They are the ones that made it because of their minds, not their bodies. And these same minds will make them successful in almost any endeavor.

RILL BAXTER QUITS TENNIS AND GOES INTO BUSINESS

Rill Baxter, one of my former Pepperdine team members, was a typical example. As a young player he was ranked among the top ten juniors in the United States and won the US national junior doubles championship, and as a college player, he was one of the best in the nation. After graduation he spent the next five years playing professional tennis, mostly at satellite events, with only modest results. He was good, but simply not good enough to make a living playing tennis tournaments. Toward the end of his pro career he had difficulty detaching from the game, even though he knew his tennis career was going nowhere, because it was the only thing he was really good at.

Rill is very conservative, and we spoke often over the years about what he should do when he quit tennis. He agonized over the decision. When should he leave the game? What business should he try? Although he is very bright, Rill had not been a great student. He had no experience in business and could not visualize how he could make it when there were so many other people better qualified than he was. I kept telling him that it didn't matter what he did. He would be successful at anything, once he took it into his mind to devote himself to it.

I knew this because I had seen Rill's character tested over the years on the tennis court. He was physically strong but not a great athlete. On the other hand, Rill was able to push himself for hour after hour on the hottest days through intense and painful workouts. He maintained his drive year after year despite heartbreaking losses, injuries, pressures to make grades, break-ups with girlfriends, and the host of other difficulties common to young men with high levels of both testosterone and aspiration. Rill was a tough boy, and, although he had no perspective on himself, he was different from most people. It was clear to me that in a competitive situation, he would eventually rise to the top.

Eventually Rill took the plunge. With substantial uncertainty and misgivings, he began interviewing stock brokerage firms, ultimately landing a job with Solomon, Smith, Barney in their training program. Rill got his license and started at the absolute bottom of the barrel, making cold calls on the telephone. Solomon, Smith, Barney provided him with lists of prospects, and Rill tried to sell them stocks that were recommended by his research department. Few activities are more difficult. People may hang up on you, abuse you, or just play with you with no intention of buying. It takes tremendous courage to face the daily rejection, and many young brokers drop by the wayside during this process.

But this is exactly where Rill shines. He got good in tennis because he doesn't like losing, so he wasn't about to quit and lose at selling stocks either. As a tennis player, he was a fanatically hard worker and could force himself through long, unpleasant drills. And it was no different with the phones. He stayed on them longer than anybody else, learning how to sell the hard way. Rejection was his constant companion, but it could not drive him away from the phones. By trial and error Rill taught himself what approach would be effective in particular situations with different types of people. He was alert and diligent and learned to read the vocal nuances of his clients. He knew his facts well and was quick and reliable at supplying clients with information. He understood that he was young and inexperienced, so he did not attempt to act as a stock analyst himself. But he was tireless at passing on recommendations and data from his research department. He understood his own strengths and weaknesses and never pretended to be something he wasn't. Most of all, Rill was honest and persistent.

In time, people began to like and trust him. At the end of his first year, Rill was in the top five percent of his group in sales volume and money under management. At the end of seven years, Rill is one of the top brokers in his company. With a vast base of customers, Rill has hired an assistant, is making an impressive and growing amount of money, and is well on his way to figuring out the world of business, much as he did the world of tennis.

THE OTHER TEAM MEMBERS ALSO SUCCEED

And Rill is far from unique among my former Pepperdine tennis team members. Within ten to fifteen years of leaving tennis, virtually every one of them that went into business has been extraordinarily successful. For example, Sivig Suresh also went into the investment business—cold calling to begin with—like Rill. He now lives in a big house in Bel Aire and has donated a tennis stadium to his old alma mater, Pepperdine. Egan Adams started out working at a gas station in the Florida Keys and is now the wealthy owner of a huge combination marina/gas station in a prime area of Sarasota. When he left school, Rolando Vasquez was given a job at the bottom in his family's small rum importing business in Miami. Shown no favoritism, he learned the business sweating it out as a common laborer. Within fifteen years, he and his cousin had bought the entire business, Rolando's share of the cost coming largely from an immensely profitable and growing cigarette importing and distributing company that he started on the side. Leo Palin started working at McDonald's in his native Finland. Fifteen years later, he owns three McDonald's franchises and has been named to the Board of Directors of McDonald's, Europe.

None of this could have happened if these players had been unwilling to forego the quick rewards of teaching tennis. Instead, they girded themselves for the long haul where, for little pay, they learned the intricacies of their businesses from the bottom up.

SUMMARY

Success is seldom immediate. The short path rarely leads to great rewards. To reach your goals, you must be prepared to invest your most strenuous efforts and receive little in immediate return. The returns will eventually come—just not as soon as you might wish. Fortify yourself against the interim self-doubts that may arise by focusing on excellence in your day-to-day activities. Take pride in the process of achieving that excellence, stay alert, and your voyage will be pleasant and productive.

INTELLECT OVER EMOTION

The champions' intellects hold the balance of power over their emotions, so they respond to situations practically rather than emotionally.

Champions have control over their emotions rather than the other way around. They respond to problems with their logic systems rather than their emotional systems. Competitive situations in business and sport generate a host of strong emotions, some of which can hinder or even demolish one's ability to reach one's goals. Fear of failure is the major culprit, accompanied, in many cases, by its usual counterproductive cohorts—insecurity, discouragement, frustration, and urges to increase one's importance and fortify one's fragile ego. Working behind the scenes, these emotions can fog peoples' minds and lead them to make faulty decisions.

In sports, the losers become immersed in these emotions, are swept hither and yon, and their performance deteriorates. For example, the losers are prisoners of their own performance. If they are playing well, they feel good. If they are playing badly, they feel bad. This is an unstable situation in that bad play generates bad emotions that, in turn, generate further bad play. When champions are playing badly, they are practical and use their emotions to help them play better. They discipline their emotions to serve their purposes rather than, as most people do, allow their emotions to control them.

Consider the situation where a tennis player is behind 0–40 in a game. The average player senses that the game is probably lost and becomes discouraged. He often takes the next point lightly, tries a low percentage shot, misses, and loses the game. Jimmy Connors, on the other hand, used to psych himself up for a comeback. He understood clearly that it is disadvantageous to let the game go easily. He knew that if he put 100 percent effort into the next point, there was some small chance that he could eventually win the game, and he never willingly gave away this opportunity. He began to think aggressive, positive, courageous thoughts to induce a flow of adrenaline. He often gestured to the crowd to gain their support, which also created in him the emotions he needed. He knew that his game would follow his feelings and that good feelings would make him play better. He was completely aware of what these good feelings were and of how to get them, and he made sure that he got them before the next point started.

Connors and the other champions are practical and use everything in their power, including emotion, to help them achieve their goals. They clearly identify problems and zero in on the best approaches for solving them. The losers seem to function in a fog. They allow fears, discouragement, and other destructive emotions to confuse them and ruin their judgment. When this happens, they are as likely to adopt hopelessly counterproductive procedures as productive ones.

NANCY FOX KNOWS HOW TO HANDLE EMOTIONS IN BUSINESS

My wife, Nancy, is masterful at controlling her emotions in business situations and is the ultimate pragmatist when it comes to meeting her objectives. She spent many years behind the counters of her retail businesses and, during this time, faced thousands of unreasonable customers (mixed in, of course, with the many thousands of reasonable ones). Some were angry over trivial mistakes and made outlandish requests for retribution. Others were prepared to complain about anything short of perfection. Instead of allowing herself to become upset or getting her back up about who was in the right, Nancy handled them all intelligently and well. She was always friendly and sympathetic, never reacting negatively or emotionally, no matter how nasty, self-centered, or outrageous a customer might be. Her approach was to listen carefully to their complaints, apologize, and give them what they wanted—even if the customer was 100 percent in the wrong and it cost her money.

Nancy told me that she was able to handle these people by assuming that their aggressive remarks were not personal, as much as they might appear to be. This allowed her to resist reacting defensively. If she were to feel and display negative emotions, she would alienate customers and hurt her business. Nancy was not about to do this. Her objective was simple—make them happy so they will keep coming back and say positive things to their friends. Nancy said she tried to kill them with kindness and, in so doing, was often able to turn the angriest, negative customer into a rabid, vociferous supporter.

She was also intelligent enough to keep me out of these situations. She knows I am competitive, prone to argue, like to be right, and potentially antagonistic if an angry person who is totally in the wrong gets in my face. I can recall one situation in our Encino, California, restaurant, insignificant as it may be in the greater scheme of things, that irritated me so much that I had to leave before I said something I shouldn't.

In our shopping area we had bins of hard candy for sale. A lady was waiting for a table, and her young child was running loose. His first move, naturally, was to run over to our candy bin, stick in his little paw, and help himself to a fistful. His mother just stood there. He ate the first batch and went for a second. The mother still did nothing. Meanwhile I was fighting for control. "Hey lady," I wanted to say. "We are in business here, and, believe it or not, we actually sell that stuff to pay our bills!" But I bit my lip and kept my mouth shut. Finally, the lady picked the kid up, I assumed to keep him away from our candy. But no, she lifted him up so he could get into one of our higher bins that he couldn't reach from the floor. That drove me out of the restaurant. Luckily, I was not forced into this situation often, but, just for the record, if my living depended upon it, I would darn well have learned to handle these customers with kid gloves also.

UNDERSTAND YOUR OWN EMOTIONAL WEAKNESSES

Human beings are supposed to be rational creatures, and our actions are assumed to be controlled by our conscious thought processes. Our emotions are supposed to serve our rational brains. Fortunately or unfortunately, the reverse is more frequently the case. We often want to do things for emotional reasons. Then we use our reasoning to justify and backup our emotions. Attaining practical goals in business is substantially easier for those who clearly understand their own emotional make-ups. They know what to be wary of.

For example, I have already admitted to my own competitiveness. I always take this into account when I enter into business negotiations. I know I have to watch myself. Before I start I have some idea of the minimum deal that I believe to be acceptable, but as the process unfolds, each side sets forth proposals and counterproposals. Things change. New factors and deal structures appear. Before it is over, proposals that I may have originally considered unreasonable, will sometimes, in the light of new information, actually be reasonable and acceptable. But I have to watch myself. I have learned that the interplay of negotiation starts to strike me emotionally as some sort of a competitive game, and I start wanting to win. I feel like I don't want to give in. Like a tennis match, I want my opponents to capitulate, which they are not usually about to do. The danger is that my emotional proclivities will harden my position unrealistically, and I will blow the deal by yielding to my inclination to play hardball. When I get to this stage, I slow down and think things over or discuss the situation with a level-headed associate. I make every effort to remove my own emotions from the equation and come up with a reasonable and workable deal. Only then, with a foot firmly on my competitive instincts, do I make final decisions.

ALLOWING EMOTION TO TRUMP REASON IN INTERPERSONAL RELATIONS OFTEN LEADS TO DISASTER

In no other realm are we in greater danger of casting aside sound rational judgment in favor of emotion than in interpersonal relations. Social beings that we are, a great number of our emotional needs involve other people. And many of these needs are so extraordinarily powerful that it is the rare person who can muster sufficient reasoning and willpower to overcome them. If you want examples of this in action, tune in any day to the "Dr. Laura" talk show on the radio. A caller will complain that her live-in boyfriend cheats on her constantly, staggers home drunk a couple of times a week, beats her up, and sponges off her money—but she loves him. "What should I do?" the caller will ask. Dr. Laura exerts iron self-control to resist her urge to shake the woman until her teeth rattle and responds, "DUH! GET RID OF HIM." This advice is obvious to everyone on the planet except the caller, whose rational brain is on sabbatical in Bulgaria.

Another example surfaced recently when an acquaintance of mine (lets call her Sandra) poured out the story of her crumbling marriage. She had married Philip (not his real name) sixteen years previously. Before getting married they had been friends. Both were adventurous and enjoyed motorcycle riding and scuba diving, so they hung around and had fun together. It was easy to see why Philip might be attracted to Sandra. She was (and is) bright, caring, industrious, generous, and selfless. In sum, she was very easy to be with—an excellent companion.

But there were reasons why marriage to Philip might not be advisable. Although Sandra was attractive, she tended to carry an extra ten to fifteen pounds of weight, and this always disconcerted Philip, who was a fitness fanatic and kept himself in perfect condition. He was always after her to lose weight, but she never did. Though both were in their middle thirties at the time, Philip was not ready to marry. He was well educated, but was neither established in his profession nor was he highly ambitious to get to work and become established. He was having too much fun working out, riding his bike, and taking care of himself. Cold and self-centered, Philip had no great urge to give up his freedom, no great urge to start thinking "we" instead of "I," and no great urge to embark on the grind of supporting a family.

Sandra had a different agenda. Her biological clock was ticking and she wanted a child. Since she was always deeply considerate of the needs of other people anyway, marriage was a natural progression for her. Besides, she loved Philip and wanted to be with him. In time, she thought, his love for her would grow as would his attachment to a young and expanding family, even if it wasn't as strong as it might be at the beginning. She became pregnant and Philip married her.

For fifteen years the marriage simply endured. It never evolved into the powerful, communal, loving partnership that Sandra had envisioned. Philip was never satisfied—focusing on Sandra's faults, continuing to complain about her few pounds of extra weight, and continually looking out the window at what he might be missing. All along the couple struggled with money—both working full time—and shared responsibilities for raising their two children. Philip respected Sandra and realized that she was a good person, but he did not appreciate and love her in the way necessary to create a happy union. There was little fun in the marriage and little overt affection either. Instead there were the usual grown up hardships—responsibility, work, and stress.

Then Sandra learned that Philip had, for some time, been clandestinely seeing another woman. The girl was 12 years his junior—slim, pretty, and smitten with Philip's education and apparent worldliness. For his part, Philip was swept up in reliving his days of youthful freedom and enjoying himself. Although Sandra was willing to forgive and forget, nothing she said could deter Philip from his new relationship. He packed his things and moved out.

A year later Philip was still deeply entangled with his young paramour and talking divorce. As she told me the story, Sandra was in a quandary. She recognized that her marriage to Philip had serious problems (an understatement of titanic proportions), yet during the past year she had thought it over and concluded that Philip was not totally at fault. She had not been the perfect wife either, she said. She now understood her own shortcomings and felt she could change them. Should she approach Philip, she asked, and tell him about her newfound self-understanding and desire to change? If she did this, might not reconciliation still be possible?

I was flabbergasted! Sandra's emotional system had totally shutdown her rational brain. From her standpoint, this entire marriage had been a classic case of poor judgment from start to finish, but she still couldn't see it. Because Sandra loved Philip and wanted so desperately to marry him (all emotional needs), she ignored reason, which would have told her that this marriage was a terrible idea. It was obviously doomed from the beginning because Philip was immature, not emotionally ready for marriage, and most importantly, did not want to marry her. Reason would have told Sandra that this situation was more likely to get worse than better. Unfortunately, her emotional need to formally bond with Philip overpowered rationality.

At the end of it all, Sandra still does not get it, and her thinking is still emotionally driven. She is a little overweight and insecure—afraid to be thrust out into the singles scene. To Sandra, a weak, loveless marriage is preferable to confronting her fears of ending up alone. In desperation, she hopes to hang on to a marriage that is already gone by offering to change. Despite any changes that Sandra might propose, Philip has about as much chance of coming back as he does of becoming Secretary General of the United Nations. He is gone, the marriage is over, and it has been over for a long time. She has never had a partner, except in her imagination. If Sandra thought with her head instead of her heart, she would have recognized this years ago. She had not wanted to see it because she would have then been obliged to act contrary to her emotional needs.

She will be better off without him. Once Sandra heals from the psychic trauma of the divorce, she will be free to find a new relationship with a real partner. This time, however, she had better keep her eyes open and use her head. She had better seek a partner that wants to be with her. Sandra has a lot to offer but needs a man who can see her good qualities and appreciate her. She needs one who is less self-centered and more mature. To correctly identify these characteristics, she must keep control of her emotions and allow her intelligent, rational brain to work unimpeded.

EMOTION OFTEN COLORS DECISIONS IN THE STOCK MARKET

The stock market is another venue where emotion often overpowers logic and leads the unwary to grief. The pundits say that the market is driven by greed and fear. When stocks are on the rise, and people see others raking in significant quantities of easy money, even the most conservative are eventually tempted to buy. They are greedy to get in on the easy money and fear being left behind. On the other hand, when the stock market is falling, people panic and want to sell before they lose more money. Fear rather than logic drives these sales. The emotional caldron of dealing with serious amounts of money often leads people to buy when the market is high and sell when it is low, exactly the opposite of what accurate judgment would tell them to do. These are the emotions that cause stock prices to over-react to good or bad news, tending to go up excessively on good news and fall excessively on bad. By contrast, disciplined investors resist contagion from the emotions of the herd and make decisions using only intellectual criteria. (I like the strategy employed by investment guru, Warren Buffett, whose purchases and sales are based on his analysis of the VALUE of the stock relative to its price.)

Another problem some investors have is that they cannot bring themselves to sell stocks for less money than they originally paid. Although the stock price is falling and they sense it is a dog, they grimly hang on all the way down in the vain hope that it will somehow go back up. They cannot emotionally face taking their losses. To do so means they must acknowledge their own error of judgment. They must face the fact that they screwed up—an admission of a possible character flaw? As long as they don't sell, they don't have to admit anything. Until they sell, failure is not certain, so they don't sell.

Meanwhile, investors like Buffett simply analyze the stock's value relative to its present price. If the value is less than the price, they sell. Emotion is out of the equation.

WINNERS CAN MAKE THEMSELVES DO THINGS THAT ARE UNPLEASANT

An offshoot of the champions' preference for practicality over emotion is their ability to force themselves to do things that are arduous or distasteful when their interests require it. In a sense, they are those unusual kids with willpower who can make themselves swallow bitter medicine because they know it is good for them rather than having their parents force it down their throats.

Most people know, at some level, what they OUGHT to do. They just can't make themselves do it. Their logic systems cannot overpower their emotional systems. If the task is arduous, uncertain, stressful, or otherwise disagreeable, they resist, procrastinate, delude themselves, become diverted, and end up waffling toward activities that are more appealing. These people have great difficulty doing their homework, making that unpleasant phone call, finishing projects, telling people things that may make them angry or unhappy, doing their workouts, or controlling their diets. This does not make them defective, wrongheaded, or bad. They are simply normal. That is how most people are.

Unfortunately, being "normal" in this manner is never a good thing and sometimes leads to big trouble in business. I was consulting with a bright, young gentleman last year (who I will refer to as "Greg") regarding his fledgling computer software business. Though not yet 30 years of age, Greg had worked as a computer programmer for almost 10 years. He started out by himself, doing small spot jobs for companies where he was simply paid on an hourly basis for his time. By the time I met him, Greg had his own company with gross sales of over $500,000 and was employing a half dozen people to design and install complex software systems for small businesses.

Greg was an excellent technician and an optimistic, nice guy, but he was not hardened to the pitfalls of running a small business. He had the youthful tendency of thinking with his heart instead of his head. Like most of us, Greg did not like confrontation. He shrunk back from telling people things that they didn't like to hear. Because he was afraid of adverse reactions, he could not force himself to take certain business positions with his customers that practicality would have demanded. Predictably, trouble followed.

For example, Greg did not have the stomach to appear as if he distrusted his customers. This fear made him reticent to ask his big customers for advance payments, progress payments, or other payments that would have protected him from collection risks. I advised him to insist on progress payments and to, under no circumstances, hand over the program, in its entirety, to the customer without having collected sufficient funds to at least cover all of his costs. This is because once the customer has Greg's program installed, up and operating, Greg has no recourse in the event of nonpayment other than a lawsuit. And with a small company like Greg's, he lacks the time and resources to fight for a couple of years over an unpaid bill.

Despite hearing this advice and intellectually understanding that it could protect him, Greg lacked the willpower to take an action that was emotionally distasteful. So he convinced himself that his own method was working, and he continued to put himself at risk. For awhile he got away with it. Recently, however, the inevitable occurred. A customer who owed Greg $45,000 for a completed program began to stall on payment. He had plausible excuses and paid Greg a few thousand dollars here and there to pacify him, but three weeks ago Greg read in the newspaper that his customer was laying off virtually all of his work force. Greg's phone calls to the customer over the past weeks have remained unanswered, and Greg is distraught as he contemplates the disintegration of most of his year's profit!

Greg is a normal young man who has difficulty overcoming emotion (fear of disapproval) and forcing himself to act upon practical business logic. But in order to be successful, he will have to learn, and the sooner he does, the less painful lessons he will experience. By contrast, the champions are abnormal in that their instinctive practicality can overpower their counterproductive emotions. They can force themselves to do whatever serves their purposes. You can probably imagine what Jon Douglas looks like today, at age 65—slim, active, well-dressed, not a hair out of place, and in perfect condition. He would like to stuff himself on rich foods, but resists because he does not want to get fat. He would like to lie around more and watch sports on television, but he won't because he wants to stay fit. And, like Greg, he would like to be perceived as a nice guy, but you can bet he didn't get enormously wealthy by letting his customers run off with his pocketbook. None of this is normal. Call it "strength of purpose," "self-discipline," or even "character," but it largely amounts to the triumph of will and logic over emotion. Whatever it is, the champions have it, and the rest of us must focus on it and learn how to do it.

SUMMARY

Beware of your emotions lest they distort your reasoning and lead you to behave unwisely. Make sure you understand your own emotional inclinations, and be suspicious of your quick decisions if emotions are involved. Emotions are often of short duration and changeable, and the facts may appear very different with the passage of a day or two. Take your time and weigh the issues carefully before making important decisions. Are your emotions mixing into the equation? If so, try to identify them and set them aside. As best you can, work only with the real issues. If you can't do this by yourself (and most of us often can't), discuss your ideas with a friend or business associate to gain perspective.

Chapter Fifteen

ENERGY

The champion has boundless
physical and mental energy.

Donald Trump, billionaire developer, entrepreneur, and media darling, was describing the type of person he was looking for to run one of his companies on his hit television show, "The Apprentice." "It's all about energy!" Trump said, meaning that he looks to hire people who are movers, not sitters; doers, not talkers. He wants to hire champions, of course, and has succinctly identified one of their key characteristics. Champions possess an extraordinary abundance of physical and mental energy.

A great deal has been written and spoken about the champion's drive, determination, will to win, or whatever else one wants to call it. (I will use these terms interchangeably in this chapter.) But none of this is meaningful without it resulting, ultimately, in ACTION, and action demands energy. Everyone wants to win. And most people think they are determined to be successful. But nothing happens until they actually do something about it. Talk is cheap. So is thinking. And wishful thinking is cheaper still.

Of course, intelligent planning and focus of energy are helpful, but we all must be wary of "paralysis by analysis," where, driven by ever-present subconscious fears of failure, planning and thinking actually replace action. Energetic champions have their insecurities too, but they keep moving forward anyway, despite their fears and, sometimes, even because of them. Elia Kazan, the great director and best selling author, was, in his youth at the Yale drama school, noted by his teachers for his "lack of visible talent," his only obvious gift being that of "excessive energy." It is this energy that impels champions to work harder than other people and do whatever it takes to succeed, including, whenever necessary, getting their hands dirty. Because their active minds constantly mull over the intricacies of their enterprises, they ultimately uncover better and better ways of reaching their goals. But this thinking occurs along with action, not instead of it.

In sports the winners eschew the couch and television set for the batting cage, the hoop at the park, the practice tennis court, or the ice rink. In business they are quick to get up from their chairs and go to meetings, visit facilities, call on clients, put together sales materials, complete their expense reports, and so forth. They enthusiastically roll up their sleeves and become physically involved in a project at the least hint that such involvement can speed the job forward. In short, they are quick to initiate action, both physically and mentally.

Their energy tempts them to jump in personally to get things done. They will depend on other people only as much as they have to. In business they are practical enough to realize that they cannot do everything themselves—yet they wish they could. (If they could magically multiply themselves a thousand-fold, they would happily dispense with employees and do it all personally.) But even when delegating, they rarely turn over crucial aspects of their businesses to subordinates without maintaining a continual grasp of important details themselves and constantly monitoring and measuring performance.

And how do the unsuccessful differ? To be blunt, many are simply mentally and physically sluggish. They move only when they have to. Getting out of their chairs is an effort, and they prefer to sit at their desks and push papers around. Going across the room to the filing cabinet is often more than they can manage, so papers tend to pile up on their desks. They procrastinate. Television is their most attractive recreation because it demands so little of them. Although they may claim otherwise, their actions do not reflect a true drive to achieve. They show no great enthusiasm for the task at hand. Rather, they plod along, doing a minimum of work, delving into projects only so deep as to pass cursory inspection, handing off responsibilities to other people whenever possible, and hoping that outside factors will move their fortunes forward.

Why is this so, since if you ask them, the unsuccessful people can talk quite as good a game of wanting to achieve and win as anyone else? In addition to simple laziness, the answer is that unconscious fear of failure saps a portion of their drive. It enfeebles them. It makes them talk instead of act. Another way of putting it is that lack of self-confidence makes people hesitant to commit themselves deeply and wholeheartedly to achieving their goals. Dolly Parton highlighted the interaction between fear of failure and drive in a recent television interview. The host asked her how she managed to elevate herself from the depths of childhood poverty and obscurity to become an international superstar? Dolly answered, "I was able to do it because I was never afraid to fail. This gave me the strength to try things and if they didn't work, to try again."

Of course, we all can be a little lazy and have, to a greater or lesser extent, these subconscious fears of failure. As a result, they subtly give us reasons for not trying new things, for quitting projects before we finish, or for hesitating because we believe that modest obstacles are insurmountable. By contrast, champions either fear failure less or are able to press on in the face of them. In one way or another, they are able to vigorously propel themselves forward. So if you find yourself sitting around and procrastinating when you should be up and energetically moving, look for the sly influence of self-doubt and give yourself a kick in the pants to get you past it.

NAPOLEON'S CAREER DEMONSTRATES THESE TRAITS IN ACTION

Leadership in war is similar to leadership in business or in any other area except that it is more stressful and difficult. The exceptional general, therefore, shares certain common traits with the successful business person, the successful coach, and any other successful leader—namely, enormous drive and physical energy. Napoleon's career, with its sharp rise and fall, makes an excellent illustration. (There are, in this discussion of Napoleon, details that those uninterested in history or great men may wish to skip. Feel free to do so. The beginning and ending few paragraphs contain the essence of the situation.)

Napoleon was one of the most magnificent geniuses to ever grace the pages of recorded history. He would certainly rank among the three or four greatest generals of all time. (Alexander was in a class by himself; Caesar was as skilled but more successful; and Hannibal, though he faced opposition that was ultimately overwhelming, was equally gifted.) But in addition to his military talents, Napoleon was also an extraordinary statesman, lawgiver, administrator, and organizer. Under his direction as First Council and later, Emperor, France ran with unparalleled efficiency and enjoyed widespread prosperity.

Chapter Fifteen

It is instructive to compare his first campaign in Italy, which was devastatingly successful, to his last, which culminated disastrously at Waterloo. In these two cases his differing approaches to leadership in battle drastically affected his fortunes—namely, the older Napoleon lost his youthful energy and personal attention to crucial details.

Napoleon's early military accomplishments were made possible, despite enormous disadvantages in manpower and material, by his driven, relentless, almost superhuman energy and towering intellect. He was up early, before his troops, in the saddle and riding incredible distances to gather information with his own eyes. He moved tirelessly all day long, was everywhere, and became intimately familiar with all necessary details. He depended on no one but himself, and in this way could accurately assess the state of affairs and, with his brilliant intelligence, make correct decisions. The result was victory after victory.

His first command, in 1796 at the age of 27, was of the French army in Italy—a rag-tag, half-starved collection of troops that was heavily outnumbered by its well-equipped Austrian-led enemies. The French army's experienced and older officers looked askance as their new commander approached—short, pale, and all but unknown. In short order they were brought to heal by the master's hand. He was such an obviously superior human being that one tough, grizzled general remarked that the intensity of his gaze was so penetrating that it actually made him tremble.

Napoleon's 37,000 men were outnumbered two to one, yet he had boiled down battle strategy to the simple maxim that "God is on the side of the heaviest battalions." This meant that he would win the battle if he could concentrate more men at one point than his enemy, regardless of the fact that the enemy might have more forces overall than he did. To succeed, this strategy required speed of movement, energy, good information, and deception. In fact, general Nathan Bedford Forrest, the greatest Southern cavalry commander of the American Civil War, reputedly summed up his own success with the same strategy as, "Git thar the fustest with the mostest."

Fortunately, the Austrian line was widely strung out, and by striking it in the center, Napoleon was able to separate the 25,000 Piedmontese (Austrian allies) on the right wing from the 35,000 Austrians on the left. He planned to beat each separately with his 37,000 men, starting with the largest, which were the 35,000 Austrians. In a flurry of ferocious and rapid activity, Napoleon drove the allies apart, won battle after battle, and in less than two weeks was victorious everywhere. He immediately followed this up by marching north and frightening the King of Sardinia into signing an armistice, which left him free to turn on the balance of the Austrian army. With a series of incredibly swift maneuvers (marching with a fleetness of foot not seen since the time of Caesar), he overwhelmed the Austrians (culminating in his awe-inspiring victory at Rivoli, where, with 30,000 men he took 20,000 prisoners) and drove the Austrians out of Italy.

By 1815, as he approached the battle of Waterloo, Napoleon was a changed man. The years of stress had taken a tremendous physical and mental toll. His stomach and liver were diseased, sapping his strength and dissipating his bionic energy. He had become fat, pleasure loving, and unwilling to face discomfort and bad weather. Equally important, his confidence had undoubtedly been shaken by the events that led up to the loss of his throne two years previously.

Then Napoleon had blundered in pursuing a hopeless guerilla war in Spain that drained his army's resources and undermined its morale, followed by his debacle in Russia, where the flower of his Grande Armee had been destroyed in its disastrous retreat from Moscow. He had miscalculated fatally when, in the ominous shadow of the approaching Russian winter, he had continued advancing on Moscow, assuming that the Russians would sit still until he got there and surrender. They didn't. Instead, after evacuating and burning Moscow, they simply let him have it. Then they waited for him to run out of food in the burned-out city and retreat. When he finally did, they chased and annihilated his starving, freezing troops.

Although at the time of Waterloo he talked as confidently as ever, these losses must surely have made Napoleon more fearful of failure than he was during his earlier days of unbridled success. This, combined with his loss of physical energy, made Napoleon more hopeful than careful and more readily inclined to trust his fate to luck. He tried to make up for omissions and oversights with spectacular strokes. Rather than obtaining information personally from the saddle, he began to spend more time in his tent and to rely on subordinates for important details and on unsubstantiated assumptions. He commanded from headquarters rather than the front. All this led to disaster at Waterloo.

The situation at Waterloo was similar to the one Napoleon faced in Italy in 1796. He had 125,000 troops under his command and faced the allied armies of Wellington (England) with 124,000 men and Blucher (Prussia) with 95,000. His plan was the same as before and just as excellent—strike at their center, separate the allies, drive them apart, and defeat each singly, starting with the largest.

Napoleon started eagerly and early and drove his army, against light opposition, to a position between the allies. Wellington, in an inexplicable blunder, had not yet arrived, and Napoleon easily forced Blucher eastward, away from Wellington. Then, overcome by physical exhaustion, he retired to rest overnight in a small town in the rear. Days passed as Napoleon regained his strength, reconnoitered the battlefield, and consulted with his aides. Instead, he should have immediately pursued Blucher, driven him further east, kept an eye on him with a small force, and then dealt immediately with Wellington before the English commander had time to prepare. But he had lost much of his physical energy, leading to the omissions and sluggish actions that insured his defeat.

As he approached Wellington, Napoleon did not know exactly where Blucher was. He assumed that Blucher was where he wanted him to be. In the old days he would have ascertained such a vital piece of information with his own eyes, because if Blucher were able to join Wellington during the battle, Napoleon would be ruined. He had to, at all costs, ensure that this did not happen, yet he did let it happen. Blucher showed up midway through the battle. Although Wellington had, in any case, stymied Napoleon's attacks by shrewdly positioning his forces behind a ridge, Blucher's arrival on the battlefield guaranteed Napoleon's defeat. Because he had lost the physical energy, intimacy with vital details, and drive of his youth, Napoleon spent his remaining few, sad years imprisoned on an isolated, unhealthy, miserable rock named St. Helena.

MY TENNIS COACHING EXPERIENCE AT PEPPERDINE

By the same token, I have seen success and failure occur in my own coaching career as well as in business because of similar factors. When I began coaching the Pepperdine tennis team, it did not enjoy a strong reputation for tennis excellence. Yet I did not relish losing. I was young (relatively), strong, and eager, so I spent every evening until 8:00 PM on the phones talking to recruits, relentlessly pursuing better players. At the same time, I drove my players hard in practice. I was still young enough to play and beat most of them myself (at least for a set), so they listened when I made suggestions. I instituted a strenuous training program and took part in it myself because I wanted to get into good shape anyway. I was interested and concerned with every detail, and the team performed well. We ended the year ranked seventh in the nation, an all-time high for Pepperdine.

The following ten years were good ones for Pepperdine tennis. I continued to recruit with relentless energy and drove the team to work in practice up to the limits of their endurance. I wanted to win, and the team knew it. They responded by keeping Pepperdine ranked among the top five teams in the nation and always being a top contender for the national championship. Our school became well-known as a tennis power, and I was admitted to the Intercollegiate Tennis Coaches Hall of Fame.

Then I began to deteriorate as a coach, although I did not realize it at first. I had never intended the coaching job to be a full-time occupation, but I had turned it into one because I wanted so badly to win. Now, however, in what used to be my spare time, I became more and more deeply involved in our family baking business (which I will discuss later in this chapter). Imperceptibly in the beginning, my interest and energetic commitment to coaching began to wane, and with this, my energy and activity in recruiting and driving practice fell off.

I had worked out my systems and developed my strategies such that I thought I could maintain my results without putting in the ultimate physical and mental efforts personally. I thought I could train my excellent assistant coach to think like I did and lay off day-to-day responsibilities on him. Instead of staying late and spending time on the phones recruiting and hawking my players on the practice courts, I began relying more and more on my assistant. I left much of the recruiting to him, and I arrived at the courts only minutes before practice began and ran the program by the seat of my pants. Details slipped my mind. I did not supply personal force to the practices and matches, and the players could feel it. I was loath to discipline the players as firmly as before because, unwilling to pay the price myself, I felt morally unable to demand it of others. And the team's performance and ranking fell as a result. The team was still good, but not good enough. During this period, Pepperdine was usually ranked among the top ten teams in the nation, but at the bottom of the top ten, and it was not a serious contender for the national championship.

I eventually realized that I was kidding myself. I had not factored in the crucial value of moral force emanating from the team's leader's heavy expenditure of mental and physical energy. I made the same mistakes as Napoleon did in

167

his later years. These were: becoming physically lazy, overly dependent on sub-ordinates, too personally distant from the crucial details of running the team, and hoping for good results instead of getting involved physically myself to force good results. My payoff was the inevitable downward spiral. When this concept sunk in, I resigned as coach and was happy to see Pepperdine hire a young, hungry, aggressive, and, most importantly, energetic new coach.

THE AMBITIOUS BUSINESS PERSON MUST ALSO BE ENERGETIC

I have run a number of businesses, and, with one notable exception (which I will discuss shortly), I have been quite good at it. Some years ago I did not know why this was so, but because failure is a better teacher than success, I now know. My last entrepreneurial effort was an expensive, painful, time-consuming lesson in how NOT to run a business. Here too, I made the same mistakes as Napoleon in his later years and was fortunate that the penalty for operating a business poorly is not, as it was in his case, a one-way ticket to prison on the isolated isle of St. Helena.

Over the years I had accumulated a reasonable net worth. I was well off, not rich, but I did have enough money so that if my spending remained sensible, I would not have to work unless I chose to. I could not, by any measure, afford to throw money around, but I had enough extra capital to take a few risks. This tempted me to try a new business venture without my usual detailed research and the energy to personally work like a dog if needs be. I felt like I had too much money and was too old to kill myself working full time anymore. After my many years of experience, I had become adept at quickly understanding the essence of a business, identifying its strong and weak points, and coming up with solutions for its problems. I was an ideal consultant. My plan for the new business was to hire other people to do the day-to-day work and merely oversee the operation myself on a part-time basis. I was living a very pleasant life without working too hard and intended to continue doing so.

I was tempted into the new venture because my wife, Nancy, had proven to be a genius for developing great-tasting food and baked-goods recipes, for designing gorgeous packaging, and, most importantly, for knowing what people want. Our most recent business before this was a chain of bakeshops and a delivery gift business, called Mrs. Beasleys. Starting in 1980, Nancy had come up with the idea of sending beautiful baskets of fresh-baked muffins, cookies, and brownies as gifts. As the first person to commercially bake and sell mini-muffins, she made them the trademark of her baskets.

Her luscious baked goods and elegant looking baskets caught on in the Los Angeles entertainment community. Mrs. Beasleys became (and still is) the "gift to give" in Los Angeles, and her customers were a "Who's Who" celebrity list, including the likes of Johnny Carson, Barbra Streisand, Bette Midler, Demi Moore, Mike Ovitz, Henry Winkler, and all the major studios, including Disney, Paramount, Warner Brothers, and Universal. She even delivered a basket to the home of Ronald Reagan when he was a sitting President. As one of the originators of the muffin craze of the early 1980s, Mrs. Beasleys was written up in *USA Today*, *Woman's Day*, *Bon Apetit* and a host of other magazines. It was a highly visible little company.

I ran company operations, oversaw its expansion into multiple units, and eventually negotiated its sale to an investment company. I ran it tight. I was brimming with energy, on top of every number, and personally involved with every problem. As a result, Mrs. Beasleys was highly profitable, and I eventually became highly overconfident (as well as lazy).

A short time after selling Mrs. Beasleys, Nancy and I went on a low-fat diet and combed the markets to find anything that tasted edible. There was precious little. Nancy was sure she could do better. With time on her hands, she started experimenting with low-fat foods and desserts. Before long she came up with a stack of fantastic recipes, tested them out on family and friends, and was gratified and excited by the rave reviews. There was nothing on the commercial market that was even close. Since we were entrepreneurs, this suggested a business opportunity that was too good to pass up, and we started Nancy's Healthy Kitchen.

Nancy conceptualized a restaurant that served uniquely delicious low-fat foods, with room set aside for a shopping area that would carry the best low-fat commercial items as well as her own line of low-fat cookies, muffins, and gift baskets. The restaurant would provide a constant flow of customer traffic for the shopping area. Nancy's plans also included a catalog gift business and a line of her own packaged low-fat cookies. These would be used in her gift baskets, sold in the restaurant, and sold wholesale to other retailers. We hired an energetic, ambitious young man who had worked for us at Mrs. Beasleys and who had some restaurant experience to run the day-to-day operations. Nancy was the creative force, and I was the part-time business consultant, overseer, and chief check-writer. So we were in business.

Our company grew rapidly because Nancy had gauged the market with deadly accuracy and our products were uniquely good. Within the first year we doubled the size of our Encino restaurant, its popularity boosted by *Los Angles Magazine's* calling it the "Best Healthy Restaurant" in Los Angeles, and its many celebrity customers, among whom were Kirsty Alley, Howie Mandel, Richard Mosk, and John Ritter. Meanwhile, Nancy's gifts attracted clients like Steven Spielberg, Dick Clark Productions, Clint Black, Tom Arnold, and Oprah Winfrey. In fact, Oprah liked Nancy's cookies so much that she invited Nancy to Chicago in December of 1997 to appear on her television show featuring "Oprah's Favorite Gifts." Our company was written up favorably in magazines such as *Bon Apetit*, *Travel and Leisure*, *Men's Fitness*, *Self*, *Shape*, and the *Los Angeles Business Journal*. In addition, Nancy developed a line of low-fat salad dressings that tasted better than most of the commercial high-fat dressings. We began to bottle and sell them in our restaurant as well as in higher-end supermarkets in the Los Angeles area.

These were heady times. The company was getting widely publicized on television and in newspapers and magazines. We were further encouraged because sales kept going up, our product lines kept expanding, and we were attracting an ever greater following of customers. But operations never ran as smoothly as we had hoped. Along the way, we had replaced our head of operations several times with people of greater and greater restaurant experience. We never really got a secure handle on running the company. We thought we could ultimately cure this by investing more money and hiring better operating people. Meanwhile, Nancy and I persistently tried to distance ourselves from the day-to-day, menial tasks that running a small company entailed.

Encouraged by our company's success, we planned a second restaurant in Beverly Hills and hired a new head of operations, who had a big resume and substantial experience in running multiple restaurant units. Then the real trouble started. We left the planning, construction, staffing, and training for the new restaurant in Beverly Hills completely in the hands of our newly hired head of operations, and, equally completely, he bollixed it up. We opened to standing-room-only crowds with improperly trained cooks, with cashiers that couldn't work the registers, with registers that didn't function properly, and with managers who didn't know what they were doing. It was a mess. Nancy spent the next three months trying to control the damage, but we still engendered a horde of disgruntled customers.

Three more heads of operations came and went. None were able to straighten the restaurant out. Even still, Nancy and I were never willing to totally engage ourselves in the business and devote the next several years of our lives making it run properly. So costs remained high and out of control while continued mistakes irked and, ultimately, drove off our customers. Our original restaurant in Encino, left to fend for itself during this debacle, began to slip as well, and the business hemorrhaged money. Faced with this catastrophe, we had no options but to sell out and take our losses. We broke the company up and sold the pieces to several investor groups.

Experience is a great teacher. The only problem with learning this way is that first you get the test, then you get the lesson. The other way round is less painful, but human nature being what it is, people naturally gravitate toward learning the hard way. We got the lesson.

First, we learned that business success depends far more on good management than on wonderful products. A well-managed business can succeed even with mediocre products, but a poorly managed business will fail no matter how wonderful the products may be.

And our management problems stemmed from the fact that we did not want to dive into the business full time and run it ourselves. This would have taken more physical and mental energy than we were prepared to commit. We lacked the willingness to make the ultimate physical sacrifices that were required. I did not have the energy and drive to spend months cooking, cashiering, cleaning, and working on the production line. That is what I would have had to do to understand the business properly. Then I could have told the employees exactly what to do and could have monitored their performance at a distance with a good system of accounting and reporting. This would have been possible because I would have known the basis for every number.

Instead, Nancy and I were only too happy to delegate responsibility to others. We wanted them to build our business for us. We did not want to get our hands dirty doing it ourselves. We depended on employees to do the ground level organization of the company, and they did it very poorly. We were capable but not willing, they were willing but not capable.

This is a serious problem because in a well-run business, security comes from having operations organized efficiently from the bottom up. The important part of a business is where the "rubber meets the road"—the specific functioning of each person and each part of the business. These must be organized, choreographed, and mapped out in detail so that everyone knows what to do and does it in the most efficient way possible. And this understanding and direction usually comes from intelligent, highly motivated owners who have done all the jobs themselves. You must have personal experience and knowledge yourself before you can tell someone else exactly what to do. (That is why McDonalds insists that store managers go through the ranks first and have personal experience cooking, serving, cleaning, cashiering, etc.) Nancy and I did not do this.

On top of this, our employees could feel the paucity of our energy and moral commitment to our business. Consequently, we did not get maximal efforts out of them. There was constant inefficiency, mismanagement, and slippage. If we didn't care that much, they certainly weren't going to care that much. Unwilling to pounce on problems ourselves, we subconsciously hesitated to monitor our employees closely, lest we uncover information that would compel us to forego our coveted leisure. We traded wishful thinking for action and were slow to move. By the time we did, the problems had, like an aggressive cancer, grown past our ability (and willingness) to control.

As in battle, the keys to running a successful business are boundless physical and mental energy resulting in: (1) a willingness to work hard and long, (2) fingertip knowledge of all significant business details, and (3) careful and frequent performance monitoring of all important subordinates. (For an analysis of the business value of controlling costs vs increasing sales volume, see Appendix 6.)

ENERGY AND DRIVE IN ATHLETICS

In sports the importance of energy, drive, and the will to win have been discussed so much that I am almost embarrassed to add my two cents. But for completeness, here goes.

Successful athletes certainly have extraordinary energy, and this powers all else. It powers the monomaniacal drive to work hour after hour, year after year on their sports and to think of little else, thereby becoming unusually alert to helpful techniques and strategies. It propels them past failures and obstacles. It increases their concentration, helps them focus, and allows them to force their bodies beyond exhaustion and pain. Without this will, no amount of physical athletic ability can make them into champions.

When I was coaching at Pepperdine, well-meaning people would tell me about young aspirants that they thought were going to be the next Rod Laver or Andre Agassi. They would say, "This guy is incredible! He is quick as lightning, serves bombs, and hits the ball like a gorilla." I would then, rather simple-mindedly, ask, "What's he ranked?" They would answer, "Oh he's not ranked at all, yet. He hasn't been all that interested in playing a lot of tennis tournaments, but with his talent, I'm sure you can make him into a great player." My answer was always, "Forget it! You are mistaking reflexes and foot speed for talent. He has no talent at all. Real talent STARTS with energy, drive, and the will to win. Without deep, burning drive, he can never get great."

SUMMARY

Whether it is in business, sports, or any other area, great success is rarely possible unless the individual possesses exceptional physical and mental energy and is action oriented. This powers the drive to win and succeed. How do you know if you are lacking these? Be suspicious if you hesitate getting up from your desk to put papers in your filing cabinet. Wonder about yourself if you would rather linger over lunch than make an extra sales call. Get nervous if you watch others getting ahead, and you spend more time bemoaning your fate and resenting their good fortune than you do striving to improve your own position.

Set small goals and get moving to achieve them. Determine at all costs to be active and to get things done, because staying where you are is the road to discontent. Success of any kind is essential for allaying debilitating self-doubts, damping subtly paralyzing fears of failure, overcoming inertia, and enhancing your drive and enthusiasm for achievement. We are all "feeling" creatures, and strong, positive, confident emotions stimulate creativity and excite our brains to make us better than we were. Small victories spawn the energy and confidence we need to achieve greater ones. Success greases the wheels of success and drives the process. Inertia and sloth kills it.

WHAT DOES IT ALL MEAN?

*We need, above all,
intelligent balance in our lives.*

W**e have covered a great deal of ground in the previous fifteen chapters. Let us now attempt to gain a more digestible perspective.

AN OVERVIEW OF "THE GAME" OF LIFE

It is clear that human beings are, by genetic predisposition and societal conditioning, propelled both to compete with each other and be productive. Winning and success in these endeavors not only elevates our status relative to others, but also engenders some level of emotional fulfillment. At the same time, the processes of competition and achievement engender fears, often subconscious, of failure, of losing, of being deficient in some mysterious character trait vital for success. It is generally these pernicious fears and uncertainties that cloud our minds and tempt us to adopt impaired strategies—strategies that simply don't work. For those of us who are not naturally as successful as we might like, the second section of the book provides remedies—strategies that do work.

Of the various attributes possessed by the champions that make them so successful, one might well wonder which of them is the most important. The answer is easy—high mental and physical energy, as described in Chapter Fifteen. This translates into extraordinary drive, will, and commitment, without which the other success strategies have no force and little value. Unfortunately, this attribute is, in the general population, all too rare.

What makes me think so? Some evidence appears in the fact that pushy, aggressive, over-the-top parents have reared an extraordinarily large number of successful tennis players—a much higher percentage of the total than could reasonably be attributed to chance. Most of these parents were not especially knowledgeable in tennis, though many were successful athletes themselves in other sports. What they provided for their offspring was not so much information and specific tennis-related techniques, but rather, energy and drive. All of these players were, if nothing else, fanatically motivated from the time they were very young.

Continuing, let us change gears for a moment and consider a hypothetical thought experiment. Suppose you presented me with 1,000 randomly selected young boys and girls and asked me what could I do, if I were parenting them all, to create the greatest number of tennis champions. Assume that I were further instructed to disregard any consideration of the effects such actions might have on the child's development as an emotionally balanced, well-adjusted, and happy human being. (Not something you would ever ignore when it comes to your own kids or any kid, for that matter. But this is, after all, only a thought experiment.) Anyway, how would I proceed?

First, I would act as an over-the-top, aggressive, driven, scary parent—pushing the kids to work long, hard hours on their games and to win matches in tournaments. I would emotionally reward them for success and punish them for failure. I would promote the message that success in tennis is the object of life and that anything less than excellence is failure. This would, at the least, produce 1,000 super-motivated tennis players. Unfortunately, more than half of them would, in all likelihood, not be able to take it and would rebel, quit playing, hate the game, or become otherwise emotionally unbalanced. But some reasonable percentage of the kids would have the inner resiliency to absorb this kind of pressure without breaking down. With them I would have produced a relatively large group of youngsters who would be willing to focus all of their mental and physical resources on the practice courts for four or five hours a day. And this is where champions are produced. Out of this large, driven group I would be likely to produce several champions.

Compare this outcome to an alternative where I raise the 1,000 kids in a happy, low-pressure, balanced environment. As a reasonable individual, I would encourage them to get good grades in school, participate in team sports, enjoy their friends, and play tennis. They would be free to supply the bulk of their own tennis motivation. Bearing this in mind, how many of them, would you guess, would be tempted to single-mindedly drive themselves for four or five hours a day for ten years in hopes of becoming a tennis champion? Two? Three? Five? Who knows, but certainly not many. The extraordinary drive of champions is not naturally a widespread commodity. Most kids, oddly enough, prefer playing video games, drinking milkshakes, and watching television to spending hour after hour concentrating and sweating on a hot tennis court. The odds of producing a tennis champion with a normal, low-key upbringing are obviously very slim. And, of course, this analysis holds for almost any field of endeavor. To surpass the masses in any area ultimately requires extraordinary efforts that are often mentally and/or physically unpleasant.

Insufficient energy and drive leading to action is the most common roadblock to success in any area. If one possesses deep enough and powerful enough motivation, he or she is usually able to figure out and acquire the rest of the tools necessary for success. The driven, energetic competitors will not be deterred by setbacks. These people will force themselves past fears of failure. They will see the strategies that are working because they so badly want to reach their goals. They will learn to control emotions because they will see that rampant emotionalism blinds the intellect. And clear-eyed intellect allows us to avoid potholes on the pathway to reaching our goals. They will realize that excuses are a poor substitute for performance. In fact, all of the success strategies outlined in the foregoing chapters will eventually come into play when the driven individual puts his or her mind to the task over time. My hope, with this book, is to make it happen more quickly.

So far we have explored the reasons why we want to succeed and the strategies employed by the successful, but crucial questions remain. One of them is whether employing these strategies and becoming successful competitors and achievers will ultimately make us happy? The answer will sound like the typical psychologist's (or worse yet, lawyer's) answer—maybe. Certainly winning makes us happier than losing, and success is more pleasant than failure, but these things are only parts of the whole. If overdone, they can end up making us quite unhappy. Equally or more important are personal relationships, love, and family. And an all-encompassing compulsion for achievement that neglects or subverts family and loving personal relationships will result in unhappiness more surely than repeated failures in business or on the athletic field.

In fact, it is not uncommon for individuals whom we identify as "champions" in their chosen fields to be blindly and excessively driven such that they neglect personal relationships and end up empty and unhappy. Single-minded focus poses its dangers. Yet people need some degree of success and achievement to feel good about themselves. For this reason one may be better off learning the strategies that bring success in competition and achievement rather than being one of the born super-competitors and achievers who has never behaved in any other way. Balance, perspective, and a thoughtful approach to all of life's difficulties provide the likely path to ultimate fulfillment. And getting a few more wins and the odd bit of extra success won't hurt the process either.

APPENDIX

I. THE ROLE OF EVOLUTIONARY PRESSURE IN CREATING AGGRESSIVE, PUGNACIOUS INDIVIDUALS

Since man is, by nature, a social creature and must live communally in groups, the question arises as to why so many aggressive, suspicious, antagonistic individuals evolved? Surely these are antisocial tendencies, so what value would such characteristics have to the group?

My answer is purely speculative, but it seems reasonable to me that these people evolved in prehistoric tribal times as warriors. Why this might be so follows from an analysis of the individual's function within the group. As described in Chapter Two, the members of social species, like wolves, dogs, chimpanzees, or humans, have different temperaments because they have different functions within the group that are useful to group survival.

The pugnacious, aggressive individuals would have developed early on when men lived in small family groups, and their value to the tribe would have been in protecting the tribe from attack or even participating in attacks on others. Man is his own natural enemy. People have fought each other since the earliest times, and the strong and clever have survived. The weak and less clever have been wiped out and their territory occupied by the victors. This is an evolutionary tool that functioned to improve the species, much like lions improve the genetic fleetness, strength, and health of zebras.

NATURAL SELECTION IN ACTION

Anyone who doubts the influence of this cold-hearted natural selection process on the gene pool of human beings would do well to consider the fate of the "Tainos," those Indians who inhabited the Caribbean islands upon which Columbus first landed. They were described by the first explorers as producing plentiful crops with a minimum of labor, enjoying ample leisure, living in spacious, clean homes, and having developed a benign and harmonious society which was almost totally ignorant of war, greed, and fighting. In his letters to Ferdinand and Isabella, Columbus described them as "very gentle and without knowledge of what is evil; nor do they murder or steal." He also wrote, "They became so much our friends that it was a marvel…They traded and gave everything they had, with good will." On another occasion he said of them, "…in all the world there can be no better or gentler people…All the people show the most singular loving behavior and they speak pleasantly…I assure Your Highnesses that I believe that in all the world there is no better people nor better country. They love their neighbors as themselves, and they have the sweetest talk in the world, and are gentle and always laughing."

But Columbus and the early Spanish colonists had plans for the Tainos of a less benevolent character. Columbus saw them as weak and fit to be slaves and servants. He wrote, "they bear no arms, and are all naked and of no skill in arms, and so cowardly that a thousand would not stand against three…They are fit to be ordered about and made to work, to sow and do everything else that may be needed…because all that they are ordered to do they will do without opposition…."

The Spaniards proceeded to kidnap, enslave, rape, and murder the gentle, helpless Tainos with a ferocity, cruelty, and callousness that defies imagination. When the Tainos, objecting to the rape of their women and pillage of their property, refused to obey the Spaniards, the Governor decided to punish them by sending out a force of 300 armored soldiers with horses, dogs, and guns. K. Sale in his book *The Conquest of Paradise* describes what happened when the soldiers encountered a group of several thousand "gentle" Tainos: "the soldiers mowed down dozens with point-blank volleys, loosed the dogs to rip open limbs and bellies, chased fleeing Indians into the bush to skewer them on sword and pike." That was only the beginning.

Forts were established across Espanola, and the gallows became the symbol of Spanish rule. The Indians were enslaved and hung, stabbed, mutilated, or burned for the most trivial of offenses. Every Taino over the age of 14 had to pay tribute in the form of a hawk's bell full of gold every three months. Those that didn't were "punished" by having their hands cut off, and, as chronicled in the journals of a Spanish witness, Las Casas, they were left to bleed to death.

It did not take long to completely dispose of the Tainos. Estimates of the Taino population in the Caribbean islands in 1492 range from 500,000 to several millions. Within 20 years it was down to 30,000 and by mid-century these lovely people were virtually extinct. Of course, disease sped up the extinction process, but the Spaniards did not need the help. It would have taken but a few extra years for them to complete the process by themselves. Such has been the fate, historically, of people too weak, gentle, or technologically backward to defend themselves.

Unfortunately for the Tainos, there was nobody to save them. In ancient times there were no policemen. Tribes had to successfully defend themselves or their genes would leave the gene pool. And success in the kind of fighting that took place then would have required individuals to have ferocious tempers and particularly violent dispositions. Warfare then was not as it is today, with people sitting on ships hundreds of miles from their targets, launching missiles, and then toggling them to their destinations while watching view screens. Even the weak and squeamish can do damage at a distance. But face-to-face physical combat required a totally different character. Who would be better at splitting someone's head open with a rock or stabbing someone with a spear—the gentle, slender, artistic ectomorph; the corpulent, pleasure-seeking endomorph; or the muscular, pugnacious mesomorph? Obviously, any tribe with a large group of mesomorphs would have been formidable in battle, and any tribe that could not defend itself was doomed to be annihilated or enslaved. John McEnroe, Jimmy Connors, Pete Sampras (who is far tougher than he appears) and their ilk may be, at times, difficult to live with, but in those days they would have been even harder to live without.

THE WINNERS AREN'T EASY TO DEAL WITH

Similarly, today's high achievers are often a mixed blessing. When I coached the Pepperdine tennis team, I constantly worked to recruit the highly ranked players. They tended to be loyal to our group and were quite good at beating up on our opponents. But many were also high-strung, did not like being told what to do, and were potentially antagonistic to me when crossed or approached wrong. And my experience with successful business people has not been greatly different. They did not get into positions of power by being pussycats. They are difficult to push around and can get as rough as necessary to accomplish their purposes.

2. PSYCHOLOGISTS TRY TO UNDERSTAND

Many psychologists have noted our powerful drive for achievement and have offered theories to explain it. The classical theories all contain grains of truth while approaching the topic from different perspectives. It is enlightening to review and compare several of these.

Sigmond Freud, the most famous name in clinical psychology, had a deficit reduction theory. He believed that we are generally driven to activity because we are lacking some necessary item, and we are, therefore, forced to work to get it. Hunger is one example. When our bodies are deficient in nutrients our blood sugar levels drop, and our nervous systems respond by making us feel hungry. The feeling of hunger activates us to seek food to reduce the nutrient deficit.

Freud also theorized that unsatisfied drives due to deficits in one area could motivate activity in another area. From this came his celebrated sexuality theories. He believed that many of our sexual needs are unsatisfied and that we are driven to reduce the resulting sexual tensions. Since we often cannot do so directly, we change focus, and the sexual drive motivates us in other areas. The great artist, for example, may be powerfully driven to create because of unfulfilled sexual needs. Freud would also have held that successful athletes or businessmen are similarly driven.

The trouble with Freud's theories, as with so many other well-publicized psychological theories, is that they are simply Freud's opinions, stemming from his personal experience with disturbed people. There is no scientific validation for them. Any confidence one might place in their accuracy simply depends on how certain one is that Freud was a genius. Of course, the argument is circular. (Freud was a genius if his theories are true and his theories are true if Freud was a genius.) Unscientific and even scary as it may seem, the argument for accepting Freud's theories is that they are true simply because Freud said so. Even scarier is the fact that this is not unusual in the field of psychology.

In fact, psychologists have fed us a diet of unsubstantiated theories for many years, and a troubling number of our accepted beliefs on education, child rearing, self-esteem, etc., are of this dubious origin. In fact, if you have a Ph.D. after your name and a glib tongue or pen, you can gather quite a following for almost any idea that has surface plausibility.

Parenthetically, Freud's sexual approach in the area of achievement strikes me as pretty shaky, as does his whole theory that unsatisfied drives in one area are transferable to other areas. But then who am I to argue with a man who looks so much more like a psychologist than I do.

ADLER HAS A DIFFERENT VIEW

Alfred Adler, an Austrian breakaway member of Freud's original inner circle, had a view that seems closer to the mark. Repudiating Freud's sexual theories, Adler theorized that man's dominant drive was for power and that this drive for power stemmed from the need to compensate for deep feelings of inferiority. It is a dark view of human nature. Haunted by insecurity, we are insatiable in our quest for power after power. Adler would have no problem explaining the behavior of Alexander the Great, Julius Caesar, Adolph Hitler, Saddam Hussein, or Bill Clinton. The rest of us would have to settle for the more mundane feelings of power that we get when we win at sports, succeed in business, or become notable in our other fields of endeavor. Power emanates from notoriety, the accumulation of money, excellence, and, as a general rule, rising above the common herd in any competitive arena. Getting ahead of other people, even controlling them, makes us feel superior, hence powerful. Adler even turned the tables on Freud and claimed that much of the lust for sex was really a lust for power.

There is little doubt that Adler was on to something. The drive for power seems to explain the competitive drive more comfortably than does Freud's sexual fulfillment theory, though it too is not a comprehensive explanation.

3. LOW STATUS WAS A SOURCE OF DISCOMFORT ON THE TENNIS CIRCUIT

Most people are more comfortable associating with others who are close to their own status. They feel diminished when they are with people of substantially higher status. For example, on the tennis circuit the players usually hang out with other players of their own level. The stars do not tend to pal around with the lower ranked players. An outsider might think that this is because the stars are aloof and feel that the lower players are not worthy of their friendship. But this is not so. The stars could, in general, happily become friends with the lower ranked players; it is the lower ranked players that have difficulty being friends with the stars. The lower players feel uncomfortable, like hangers-on or poor relations, and seek friendships with people who do not threaten their egos. Inequality of status puts the lower person at a social disadvantage, and the lower person does not enjoy this weakened position.

For the same reason, the tennis players particularly dislike losing to their friends or teammates. This is because social status among tournament tennis players is determined by who wins, and the losers are the underlings. If one must be an underling, it is more palatable to be one relative to people you do not see often. Being an underling in the group that you see every day is less pleasant. When I was playing tournaments, I would prefer to lose to a foreign player rather than to an American. If I had to lose to an American, I would prefer him to live on the East Coast (rather than my own area which is California). And my least preferred loss of all would be to one of my friends—who I would have to see all the time.

4. THE IMPLICATIONS OF SINGLE-PARENTHOOD

Common wisdom has it that boys raised only by their mothers are severely disadvantaged because they lack a male role model in the home. To back this up there are a host of statistical studies showing that boys without fathers in the home have greater difficulties in school, with the law, and earning a living than do boys from two parent families. These results are in direct conflict with McClelland's work, which would even predict that the absence of the father would give the boys a greater need for achievement rather than a reduced one.

It highlights the danger of drawing conclusions from correlations. The fact that there is a correlation between the lack of fathers in the home and achievement difficulties in boys does not mean that one causes the other. They could both be correlated with a third factor that is the real cause of both of them—the fact that too many single-parent families are headed by immature young women who have children out of wedlock or by women who are overworked and stretched too thin trying to earn a living while raising a child. It is not unreasonable to assume that: (1) women who are foolish enough to have children out of wedlock may well be foolish enough to do an irresponsible job of raising them or, (2) many single mothers who must spend too much of their time struggling to make a living do not have enough time and energy left to properly raise their children. McClelland, of course, would say that it is quite possible for a single mother to produce a high-achieving son as long as she is diligent and thorough in imparting to him a proper value system.

5. THIS IS A DIVERSION FROM OUR TOPIC OF COMPETITION, BUT AS A FREE ADD-ON, HERE ARE SOME RULES FOR MAKING CONVERSATIONS INTERESTING

Conversations will be entertaining only if:
1. They are particularly pertinent to the listener's life, because everyone is surely interested in himself or herself. This includes their business, family, etc.
2. The topics are of general interest, like sports, child development, human nature, or politics, or are those from which one can generalize and draw useful lessons or morals. To be sure you are on target, watch your listeners and note their reactions. If their eyes are getting glassy, ask them questions or change the topic.
3. They are informational and teach the listeners about something that they are interested in. (The latter restriction most certainly rules out topics like what you had for breakfast.)
4. They are funny. This always works, but is extremely difficult to pull off.
5. Your listeners get to do most of the talking. You allow them to set the agenda by asking questions about topics that may interest them.

On the other hand, conversations are sure to be deadly boring if you talk, as is incredibly common, about yourself in a sort of stream of consciousness manner that includes volumes of mind-numbing minutiae. My favorite example is when someone tells you in painful detail about a dinner he recently had at a fine restaurant. "The table setting was exquisite—beautiful ruffled linens and cute little napkins embroidered with lace flowers—blah, blah. And the food, you've never tasted anything so good. The appetizer was three kinds of cheeses melted on dark toast and topped with large, brown mushrooms and white cream sauce. blah, blah, blah." The possible tedious details are endless. And

Heaven help you if they start in on their kids! As a general rule, adjectives are tiresome. Verbs, particularly colorful action verbs, are more absorbing.

If you are bent on not only boring your listeners but also irritating them, talk exclusively about yourself, and pay particular attention to your possessions, your expensive furnishings, your good business judgment, the tasteful decorating of your home, or your canny investments in the stock market.

For perspective, think of your conversation as analogous to a home movie. It will only be interesting to outsiders if they are in it, if it contains information of general interest or significance, or if it is funny. If it shows your family having a birthday party and your viewer is not there, be sure to serve plenty of strong coffee.

6. ARE SALES IN A BUSINESS MORE IMPORTANT THAN CONTROL OF COSTS?

In any business there are two overall determinants of profit—sales and expenses. The object is to maximize sales and minimize expenses, and the excellently run businesses do both. On the other hand, most businesses are better at one than the other (Nancy's Healthy Kitchen was better at increasing sales than it was at controlling costs, although it wasn't great at either.) This is because sales and cost controls require two different mentalities, and few individuals are equally good at both. The sales personality tends to be a people-oriented believer who is enthusiastic and may even slide over a few inconvenient details, while the cost-controlling personality is likely to be more detail-oriented, precise, and conservative. The two can't be more different.

The question may be asked, "If you have to choose between them, which is more important—controlling costs or selling?" (Confusion arises because high sales can make up for a great deal of inefficiency in controlling costs.)

My experience is that cost control is primary. When costs are out of control, the business is never secure. The situation is somewhat analogous to battle tactics in that the great military leader does not move forward far without paying attention to the security of his flanks and lines of communication. Otherwise his people are exposed to attack on their vulnerable sides and to having their supplies cut off. Business people that pursue sales without having costs under secure control are subject to similar blindsided disasters. Moreover, costs can, if allowed to run rampant, rise high enough to consume all the profits, no matter how high sales become. On the other hand, if costs are controlled well enough, most businesses can make a profit no matter how low sales may be.

ABOUT THE AUTHOR

Allen Fox is a man of incredible versatility, having reached the highest levels in academia, sports, and business. He earned a B.A. in physics and a Doctorate in psychology, both from UCLA, and later taught classes at Pepperdine University in psychology and at Long Beach State University in business statistics. At the same time, Dr. Fox was competing as a world class tennis player. He won the NCAA singles, the Canadian Nationals, the U.S. National Hard-courts, reached the quarterfinals at Wimbledon, and was a three time member of the United States Davis Cup team, having been ranked as high as #4 in the United States.

After his tennis playing days ended, Dr. Fox went into business, working in the investment banking departments of two small New York Stock Exchange brokerage firms, Kleiner-Bell and Newberger-Loeb. From there he went on to manage Wyler Associates, a private investment company that owned and directly controlled a number of diverse businesses, among which were apartment building construction and management, cattle feeding, and international steel sales. Still later he was the owner and chief operating officer of several small private companies in the specialty food business.

But the energetic Dr. Fox did not stop here. He also coached the Pepperdine University tennis team, building it from a small, unknown program into a national powerhouse. His teams reached two NCAA finals and were ranked among the top five teams in the nation for 10 straight years. Among the team members that Fox coached were Brad Gilbert, the renowned coach of Andre Agassi, Andy Roddick, Kelly Jones, who now coaches Mardy Fish, and Martin Laurendeau, the Captain of the Canadian Davis Cup team.

Dr. Fox is a past editor of *Tennis Magazine* and author of two classic tennis books, *If I'm the Better Player, Why Can't I Win*, and *Think to Win*. He consults and works privately with athletes on the mental issues of competition, among them some of the most illustrious names in professional tennis, baseball, and other sports. Finally, he lectures on sport's psychology at conventions and to tennis groups around the world.

Dr. Fox lives in San Luis Obispo with his wife, Nancy, and his two boys, Evan and Charlie.

5/11 5 10/18
5 - 5/16 (discarded other grubby copy.

WITHDRAWAL